D1299493

Beverly Sills

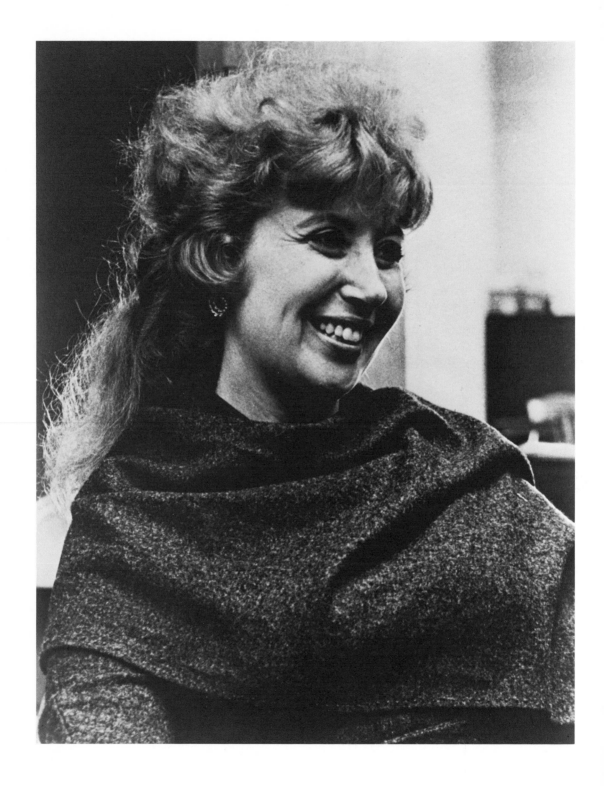

AMERICAN WOMEN of ACHIEVEMENT

Beverly Sills

BRIDGET PAOLUCCI

89-1321

CHELSEA HOUSE PUBLISHERS

NEW YORK · PHILADELPHIA

When attributed to an interviewer, material quoted in this
book is drawn from the author's interviews with Beverly Sills.

Chelsea House Publishers
EDITOR-IN-CHIEF Nancy Toff
EXECUTIVE EDITOR Remmel T. Nunn
MANAGING EDITOR Karyn Gullen Browne
COPY CHIEF Juliann Barbato
PICTURE EDITOR Adrian G. Allen
ART DIRECTOR Maria Epes
MANUFACTURING MANAGER Gerald Levine

American Women of Achievement
SENIOR EDITOR Constance Jones

Staff for BEVERLY SILLS
TEXT EDITOR Marian W. Taylor
DEPUTY COPY CHIEF Nicole Bowen
EDITORIAL ASSISTANT Claire Wilson
PICTURE RESEARCHER Patricia Burns
ASSISTANT ART DIRECTOR Loraine Machlin
DESIGNER Donna Sinisgalli
LAYOUT Design Oasis
PRODUCTION MANAGER Joseph Romano
PRODUCTION COORDINATOR Marie Claire Cebrián
COVER ART Bradford Brown
COVER ORNAMENT Winnie Klotz

1 3 5 7 9 8 6 4 2

Library of Congress Cataloging-in-Publication Data

Paolucci, Bridget.
    Beverly Sills / Bridget Paolucci.
        p.   cm. —(American women of achievement)
    Bibliography: p.
    Includes index.
    ISBN 1-55546-677-X.
        0-7910-0451-1 (pbk.)
    1. Sills, Beverly. 2. Singers—United States—Biography.
I. Title. II. Series.   89-17324
ML420.S562P36   1990   CIP
782.1'092—dc19   MN
[B]

CONTENTS

AMERICAN WOMEN OF ACHIEVEMENT

Abigail Adams
women's rights advocate

Jane Addams
social worker

Louisa May Alcott
author

Marian Anderson
singer

Susan B. Anthony
woman suffragist

Ethel Barrymore
actress

Clara Barton
*founder of the American
Red Cross*

Elizabeth Blackwell
physician

Nellie Bly
journalist

Margaret Bourke-White
photographer

Pearl Buck
author

Rachel Carson
biologist and author

Mary Cassatt
artist

Agnes De Mille
choreographer

Emily Dickinson
poet

Isadora Duncan
dancer

Amelia Earhart
aviator

Mary Baker Eddy
*founder of the Christian
Science church*

Betty Friedan
feminist

Althea Gibson
tennis champion

Emma Goldman
political activist

Helen Hayes
actress

Lillian Hellman
playwright

Katharine Hepburn
actress

Karen Horney
psychoanalyst

Anne Hutchinson
religious leader

Mahalia Jackson
gospel singer

Helen Keller
humanitarian

Jeane Kirkpatrick
diplomat

Emma Lazarus
poet

Clare Boothe Luce
author and diplomat

Barbara McClintock
biologist

Margaret Mead
anthropologist

Edna St. Vincent Millay
poet

Julia Morgan
architect

Grandma Moses
painter

Louise Nevelson
sculptor

Sandra Day O'Connor
Supreme Court justice

Georgia O'Keeffe
painter

Eleanor Roosevelt
diplomat and humanitarian

Wilma Rudolph
champion athlete

Florence Sabin
medical researcher

Beverly Sills
opera singer

Gertrude Stein
author

Gloria Steinem
feminist

Harriet Beecher Stowe
author and abolitionist

Mae West
entertainer

Edith Wharton
author

Phillis Wheatley
poet

Babe Didrikson Zaharias
champion athlete

CHELSEA HOUSE PUBLISHERS

"REMEMBER THE LADIES"

MATINA S. HORNER

Remember the Ladies." That is what Abigail Adams wrote to her husband, John, then a delegate to the Continental Congress, as the Founding Fathers met in Philadelphia to form a new nation in March of 1776. "Be more generous and favorable to them than your ancestors. Do not put such unlimited power in the hands of the Husbands. If particular care and attention is not paid to the Ladies," Abigail Adams warned, "we are determined to foment a Rebellion, and will not hold ourselves bound by any Laws in which we have no voice, or Representation."

The words of Abigail Adams, one of the earliest American advocates of women's rights, were prophetic. Because when we have not "remembered the ladies," they have, by their words and deeds, reminded us so forcefully of the omission that we cannot fail to remember them. For the history of American women is as interesting and varied as the history of our nation as a whole. American women have played an integral part in founding, settling, and building our country. Some we remember as remarkable women who—against great odds—achieved distinction in the public arena: Anne Hutchinson, who in the 17th century became a charismatic religious leader; Phillis Wheatley, an 18th-century black slave who became a poet; Susan B. Anthony, whose name is synonymous with the 19th-century women's rights movement and who led the struggle to enfranchise women; and, in our own century, Amelia Earhart, the first woman to cross the Atlantic Ocean by air.

These extraordinary women certainly merit our admiration, but other women, "common women," many of them all but forgotten, should also be recognized for their contributions to American thought and culture. Women have been community builders; they have founded schools and formed voluntary associations to help those in need; they have assumed the major responsibility for rearing children, passing on from one generation to the next the values that keep a culture alive. These and innumerable other contributions, once ignored, are now being recognized by scholars, students, and the public. It is exciting and gratifying to realize that a part of our history that was hardly acknowledged a few generations ago is now being studied and brought to light.

In recent decades, the field of women's history has grown from obscurity to a politically controversial splinter movement to academic respectability, in many cases mainstreamed into such traditional disciplines as history, economics, and psychology. Scholars of women, both female and male, have organized research centers at such prestigious institutions as Wellesley College, Stanford University, and the University of California. Other notable centers for women's studies are the Center for the American Woman and Politics at the Eagleton Institute of Politics at Rutgers University; the Henry A. Murray Research Center for the Study of Lives, at Radcliffe College; and the Women's Research and Education Institute, the research arm of the Congressional Caucus on Women's Issues. Other scholars and public figures have established archives and libraries, such as the Schlesinger Library on the History of Women in America, at Radcliffe College, and the Sophia Smith Collection, at Smith College, to collect and preserve the written and tangible legacies of women.

From the initial donation of the Women's Rights Collection in 1943, the Schlesinger Library grew to encompass vast collections documenting the manifold accomplishments of American women. Simultaneously, the women's movement in general and the academic discipline of women's studies in particular also began with a narrow definition and gradually expanded their mandate. Early causes such as woman suffrage and social reform, abolition and organized labor were joined by newer concerns such as the history of women in business and the professions and in politics and government; the study of the family; and social issues such as health policy and education.

Women, as historian Arthur M. Schlesinger, jr., once pointed out, "have constituted the most spectacular casualty of traditional history.

INTRODUCTION

They have made up at least half the human race, but you could never tell that by looking at the books historians write." The new breed of historians is remedying that omission. They have written books about immigrant women and about working-class women who struggled for survival in cities and about black women who met the challenges of life in rural areas. They are telling the stories of women who, despite the barriers of tradition and economics, became lawyers and doctors and public figures.

The women's studies movement has also led scholars to question traditional interpretations of their respective disciplines. For example, the study of war has traditionally been an exercise in military and political analysis, an examination of strategies planned and executed by men. But scholars of women's history have pointed out that wars have also been periods of tremendous change and even opportunity for women, because the very absence of men on the home front enabled them to expand their educational, economic, and professional activities and to assume leadership in their homes.

The early scholars of women's history showed a unique brand of courage in choosing to investigate new subjects and take new approaches to old ones. Often, like their subjects, they endured criticism and even ostracism by their academic colleagues. But their efforts have unquestionably been worthwhile, because with the publication of each new study and book another piece of the historical patchwork is sewn into place, revealing an increasingly comprehensive picture of the role of women in our rich and varied history.

Such books on groups of women are essential, but books that focus on the lives of individuals are equally indispensable. Biographies can be inspirational, offering their readers the example of people with vision who have looked outside themselves for their goals and have often struggled against great obstacles to achieve them. Marian Anderson, for instance, had to overcome racial bigotry in order to perfect her art and perform as a concert singer. Isadora Duncan defied the rules of classical dance to find true artistic freedom. Jane Addams had to break down society's notions of the proper role for women in order to create new social institutions, notably the settlement house. All of these women had to come to terms both with themselves and with the world in which they lived. Only then could they move ahead as pioneers in their chosen callings.

Biography can inspire not only by adulation but also by realism. It helps us to see not only the qualities in others that we hope to emulate but also, perhaps, the weaknesses that made them "human." By helping us identify with the subject on a more personal level they help us to feel that we, too, can achieve such goals. We read about Eleanor Roosevelt, for example, who occupied a unique and seemingly enviable position as the wife of the president. Yet we can sympathize with her inner dilemma: an inherently shy woman who had to force herself to live a most public life in order to use her position to benefit others. We may not be able to imagine ourselves having the immense poetic talent of Emily Dickinson, but from her story we can understand the challenges faced by a creative woman who was expected to fulfill many family responsibilities. And though few of us will ever reach the level of athletic accomplishment displayed by Wilma Rudolph or Babe Zaharias, we can still appreciate their spirit, their overwhelming will to excel.

A biography is a multifaceted lens. It is first of all a magnification, the intimate examination of one particular life. But at the same time, it is a wide-angle lens, informing us about the world in which the subject lived. We come away from reading about one life knowing more about the social, political, and economic fabric of the time. It is for this reason, perhaps, that the great New England essayist Ralph Waldo Emerson wrote, in 1841, "There is properly no history: only biography." And it is also why biography, and particularly women's biography, will continue to fascinate writers and readers alike.

Beverly Sills

Costumed as Cleopatra, Beverly Sills acknowledges cheers for her triumphant performance in Handel's opera Julius Caesar *at the New York State Theater.*

ONE

The Performance of a Lifetime

The noise in the theater sounded like thunder—loud, rolling thunder that went on and on and on. People were shouting, cheering, stamping their feet. Beverly Sills had never heard anything like it. She had received enthusiastic ovations after other performances, but nothing to match the intensity and near hysteria of this one.

For the singer, September 27, 1966, had begun like many other days. Scheduled to perform that evening, she had slept as late as she could and, to protect her voice and conserve energy, had talked very little. But when she tried to take her usual late-afternoon nap, sleep eluded her. Her mind raced with thoughts about the performance to come.

Sills knew that the music world's most prominent critics would be at the theater that evening. It was to be the opening night of the New York City Opera Company's new production of *Julius Caesar*, a rarely presented work. The evening would also mark the official opening of City Opera's new home in the New York State Theater at Lincoln Center, Manhattan's performing-arts complex.

Professionally, the New York City Opera meant everything to Sills. Here, 11 years earlier, she had received her first important break in opera, and here she had performed major roles season after season. Considered a *prima donna* (a principal female singer) at City Opera, she was known for her ability to sing a variety of roles. She had also received excellent reviews for her performances in such cities as Boston, New Orleans, Chicago, and San Antonio. But at this point in her career, Sills needed a role that would prove she had the elusive quality that distinguishes a world-class star from a versatile, reli-

Manhattan's Lincoln Center is the site of the New York State Theater, home of Sills's beloved City Opera (left); Philharmonic Hall (right); and the Metropolitan Opera House.

able, home-grown performer. Cleopatra in *Julius Caesar* was just such a role.

Like all operas, *Julius Caesar* is a drama in which the words are sung rather than spoken. This form of music theater requires singers of extraordinary skill, training, and discipline. Experts consider the role of Cleopatra, written for the soprano voice, particularly difficult to sing.

The composer of *Julius Caesar*, George Frideric Handel, was born in Germany in 1685 and lived most of his professional life in England, where he died in 1759. The composer is best known for the *Messiah*, an *oratorio* (a long religious piece for voices and orchestra) that includes the famous "Hallelujah Chorus." Before he wrote the *Messiah*, Handel spent more than 20 years composing Italian operas based on stories from mythology or ancient history. These operas, which include *Julius Caesar*, were the rage of London for a time, but their popularity waned even before Handel's death. Since then, revivals of his operas had been few and far between.

The 1966 New York City Opera production of *Julius Caesar* was staged as highly dramatic musical theater, not merely as a vehicle for vocal display. Singers in other productions of Handel's operas had traditionally assumed

15

The works of German-born composer George Frideric Handel (above) include the 1742 choral masterpiece, the Messiah, *and the opera* Julius Caesar, *written in 1724.*

rigid, formal poses suitable for a church or concert hall, but in this *Julius Caesar*, the performers were to play their roles as three-dimensional human beings, acting and interacting as real people might.

Sills was confident that she could bring Cleopatra to life and that she could master the role's *arias* (solo pieces that express a character's thoughts and feelings), which are elaborate and lie very high in the voice. She had always used the upper register of her voice easily, and the rapid passages

in the arias would give her the opportunity to demonstrate the flexibility of her voice. She had studied the part for many months and had rehearsed it for weeks. Now the long-awaited day had finally arrived. Sills's husband, Peter Greenough, had come from their Boston home to join her in New York for this special evening. The next morning, the couple would fly back to Boston and rejoin their children.

Sills entered the theater at six o'clock that evening. She always arrived at least two hours before curtain time to make sure every detail was in order. When she walked through the stage door, she felt, as she always did, that she was coming home. Greeting the entrance guard with her usual cheery "hello," the tall red-haired soprano took the elevator up to the stage level of the theater. There she began her preperformance ritual, which started with a visit to her dressing room to check her costumes. Next she visited the stage, where the scenery for that evening's performance was in place. The set for *Julius Caesar* consisted of suspended staircases and platforms. To the audience, it would look airy and innovative; to the performers, it appeared precarious, even treacherous. Sills walked up and down the staircases, back and forth from one end of the huge stage to the other. No matter how the scenery was constructed, no matter how many times she had worked in it during the weeks of rehearsal, Beverly Sills "walked the set" before every performance to make sure she would be perfectly comfortable when she appeared before the 3,000 people in the audience. Anything could go wrong onstage, and Sills intended to take no risks.

Her next move was to check her props, which included a golden sword she would carry in one of the ceremonial scenes. The company's production staff was responsible for props, but Sills left nothing to chance. She remembered all too well a performance early in her career in which she was the last-minute replacement in a minor role, that of a Valkyrie, or warrior maiden. Her costume was fitted in a hurry, and no one thought of checking her helmet for size. Much too big, it fell off and rolled across the stage during the performance, eliciting guffaws from the audience.

Satisfied that her props were in order, Sills returned to her dressing room and began to get into character. After the makeup artist applied the thick, exotic cosmetics that transformed her into Cleopatra, the soprano donned the first of the huge Egyptian-style headdresses her role required. Then, much as an athlete warms up before a game, she warmed up her voice until it felt high and light. Vocal cords are muscles. They must be stretched gently with scales and vocal exercises before a singer is in full voice. The warm-up took almost a half hour. Finally, Beverly Sills knew she was ready to perform.

The character of Cleopatra is based on the historical queen of Egypt who lived from 69 to 30 B.C.. Reputed to be

An Egyptian temple carving shows Queen Cleopatra in ceremonial headdress. Sills's 1966 portrayal of the fabled monarch made the singer an instant celebrity.

the most beautiful woman in the ancient world, Cleopatra ruled over the kingdom of Egypt with her half brother Ptolemy. The plot of Handel's three-act opera is based on Cleopatra's relationship with the celebrated Roman general Julius Caesar. As the opera begins, Ptolemy is trying to wrest the throne from his sister. The queen decides to lure Caesar into helping her destroy her brother. Disguised as one of her own servants, she meets Caesar, who is immediately charmed. When Caesar's life is threatened by Ptolemy's soldiers, Cleopatra reveals her true identity. Caesar goes off to fight his would-be assassins while the distraught Cleopatra, who has fallen in love with the Roman general, awaits news of the outcome. He returns victorious and all ends happily as Caesar and Cleopatra proclaim their love for each other, and the people hail them for restoring peace to Egypt.

The role of Cleopatra is long and challenging. The queen's arias are full of trills, rapidly sung scales, and complex melodies. Listening to a soprano sing the role is comparable to watching an acrobat perform on a high wire. Both kinds of performance require intensive training, total concentration, and absolute control; both take the performer to

City Opera's lavish production of Julius Caesar *included a large cast, an elaborate set, and dazzling costumes. It was Sills's performance, however, that made the event unforgettable.*

dizzying heights—one vocally, the other bodily.

That evening, Sills sang Cleopatra's role with incredible precision and agility. But there was more to her performance than singing the intricate arias: Beverly Sills created a living character through music. She seemed to *become* Cleopatra, conveying the many facets of the Egyptian queen's personality. She was imperious when she teased her treacherous half brother, sensual as she wooed Caesar, heartbroken when she faced the possibility that he might be killed in battle.

The soprano's great moment came at the end of the second act. Caesar leaves to fight his enemies, and Cleopatra, left alone, sings an anguished aria begging God to take pity on her and bring Caesar back safely. That aria changed Beverly Sills's life.

Called "Se pieta," the aria is both a lament and a prayer. "If you do not have mercy on me, dear heaven, I shall die," sings Cleopatra. "Give peace to my torments or this soul of mine will perish." Sills sang the entire piece as softly as possible. Because singing softly requires great breath support and control, it is extremely difficult for a singer to sustain an entire piece at that dynamic level, particularly in a large theater. Sills dared to do it. The sound of her clear soprano voice floated across the opera house like a fine silver thread, reaching the ears of all 3,000 people in the audience. While she sang, her listeners seemed to stop breathing. The only sound in the vast auditorium was Sills's voice.

When the curtain came down, the applause was thunderous. The cast had agreed not to take curtain calls until the end of the opera, but despite that, the audience continued to clap and cheer. Sills could hear the ovation back in her dressing room. She knew then that she had given the performance of a lifetime. The next morning, Sills and her husband flew back to their home in Boston. During the flight, they checked the New York newspapers to see how the critics had reacted to *Julius Caesar*. The reviews were an outpouring of praise for the soprano. The *Daily News* said she had sung "magically"; the *New York Post* called her performance "stupendous." According to the *New York Times*, "Beverly Sills as Cleopatra had a triumph. . . . She sang with melting tone and complete artistry. . . . She always has been an attractive singer, but last night she added quite a new dimension to her work."

The excitement had just begun. When Sills returned to New York four days later for another performance of *Julius Caesar*, she found her theater mailbox overflowing with fan letters. During the weeks that followed, rave reviews continued to appear. The New York *World Journal Tribune* heralded her performance, "Praise, praise, praise: Beverly Sills's queen was an absolute triumph." *Newsweek* magazine said: "The evening belonged to Beverly Sills as Cleopatra. [She] had one of those nights singers dream of. . . . Her every entrance sparked a stir of excitement in the audience."

Sills was suddenly besieged with job

offers from opera companies throughout the United States, Latin America, and Europe. Reporters called for interviews, and people on the street pointed her out as a celebrity. Opera's newest superstar was even saluted with bumper stickers that read, "Beverly Sills is a good high."

The press proclaimed her an "overnight success." To the 37-year-old soprano, this was a joke. Beverly Sills had been performing since the age of four.

Belle Silverman, born in 1929, grew up listening to opera recordings in her parents' Brooklyn home. As a child performer, she changed her name to Beverly Sills.

TWO

Born To Sing

In 1933, "Rainbow House," a New York City radio show, originated live from the studios of station WOR every Saturday morning. An hour before each weekly broadcast, a group of children gathered at the station for lessons in singing, tap dancing, and speech. A few minutes before airtime, lessons stopped. The children waited in suspense while the host of "Rainbow House," Bob Emery, decided which of them would appear on the show that day. Almost every week, one of his choices was a chubby four year old named Belle Miriam Silverman.

Born in a Brooklyn apartment, Belle was the daughter of Shirley and Morris Silverman. Her father, American-born of Romanian parents, was an assistant manager of a large insurance firm in New York. His Russian-born wife had immigrated to the United States in 1918, just after the Russian Revolution. Shirley Silverman often recalled the

difficult journey she and her mother had made to the United States, where her father was already settled. They had crossed Russia on the Trans-Siberian Railroad and had then taken a train to China, a steamer to Japan, a freighter across the Pacific to Seattle, Washington, and another train from there to New York City. Married in 1923, Shirley and Morris Silverman had become the parents of two sons, Sidney and Stanley, by the time Belle arrived on May 26, 1929.

Living near the Silvermans' Brooklyn apartment was a large assortment of relatives. Children, parents, grandparents, aunts, and uncles enjoyed weekly gatherings at which everyone indulged in fresh bagels, smoked salmon, cream cheese, and other favorite Jewish fare. On Saturdays, the boys would go out with their father, often to a baseball game. That was Shirley Silverman's day to share her interests with her

Young performers prepare to audition for a 1930s radio show. "Kiddie acts" such as Beverly's were hugely popular during the Great Depression.

daughter, which meant taking the subway into Manhattan for anything from ice-skating at Rockefeller Center to singing and tap-dancing lessons at station WOR.

Shirley Silverman was not a musician, but she realized her daughter had a special talent, that she was born to sing. WOR's "Rainbow House" seemed to offer an opportunity to develop that talent. Belle sang on the local show regularly for three years, but when she reached the age of seven, her mother decided it was time to audition for a national program: "Major Bowes' Original Amateur Hour."

One of the nation's top 10 radio shows—in an era when radio was

Americans' principal form of entertainment—the "Amateur Hour" was an on-the-air talent contest. Each week, the program's popular host, "Major" Edward Bowes, auditioned prospective contestants and picked those he liked best to appear on the show. The performer who received the most applause from the studio audience was declared the winner of that week's contest. For her audition, Belle selected an aria, the "Bell Song" from Léo Delibes's (1836–91) French opera *Lakmé*. When he heard her, Bowes was astounded: Here was a little girl who could not only sing an operatic aria but also hit the high notes as though it were the most natural thing in the world. For seven-year-old Belle, it *was* natural.

Belle Silverman had listened to recordings of arias ever since she was born. Her mother kept a record player in the kitchen, and she played operatic arias every morning as she prepared breakfast. Most of her records featured her two favorite singers, Italian-born soprano Amelita Galli-Curci (1889–1963) and French-born soprano Lily Pons (1904–76). Both performers were *coloraturas*, sopranos noted for their agile voices and their outstanding ability to sing high, extremely ornate music.

Belle, who was known to her family as Bubbles, sang along with the recordings. By her seventh birthday, she had memorized 22 arias. "I grew up listening to arias the way kids now listen to television commercials," she recalled later. "It was a matter of constant repetition; it was inside me all the time.

Beverly and Major Bowes celebrate the singer's birthday in a CBS studio. From the age of seven, Beverly appeared on Bowes's radio shows.

Lily Pons (pictured) was petite in stature but powerful in voice. Enchanted by the French soprano's singing, young Sills sought to emulate her.

When I hummed my favorite tune, it was an aria!''

Belle sang arias in French and Italian. Although she did not understand Italian, her acute sensitivity to sounds enabled her to imitate the Italian words she heard on the recordings. French was another matter. From the time she was an infant until she was six, her parents had employed a young French-woman to help care for her. As a result, Belle was fluent in French from her earliest years. When she sang French arias, she understood every word of the text.

Belle was especially fond of the ''Bell Song.'' In this aria, which she had often heard on her mother's record player, the soprano imitates the sound of bells as she tries to attract the attention of her lover in a crowded marketplace. The piece requires the singer to produce a clear, bell-like tone and to sing wide intervals high in the voice with ease. Lily Pons had made a specialty of performing it; Belle made a specialty of imitating Pons.

As soon as Bowes heard the young soprano sing the elaborate French aria, he invited her to become a contestant on the ''Amateur Hour.'' The performer had by now changed her name to Beverly Sills on the advice of a family friend who thought it sounded more professional. For her first appearance on Bowes's show, she sang another difficult piece: ''Caro nome,'' an aria by Italy's great operatic composer Giuseppe Verdi (1813–1901). The audience's overwhelming applause made Beverly Sills the winner of that week's contest. Recognizing a crowd pleaser when he saw one, Major Bowes invited the youngster to become a regular guest on his other nationwide radio show, "Major Bowes' Capitol Family." On this program, heard by millions of Americans each Sunday evening, Beverly both sang and chatted with Bowes in her animated fashion. "I was always," she later said, "a compulsive talker."

In her 1987 autobiography, *Beverly*, Sills recalled discovering what it meant to have fans. During one "Capitol Family" broadcast, Bowes mentioned that he had given Beverly a figurine of a little white elephant for good luck. Within a week, the young girl received hundreds of small elephant statues in the mail. Soon afterward, Bowes told the audience about a dress Shirley Silverman had made for her daughter. Beverly quickly added: "My mommy won't make me a long dress, and I want one. Mama says little girls shouldn't wear long dresses, and I'm very upset." Before the week was over, dozens of long dresses had arrived at the studio in packages addressed to Beverly Sills. Once she had learned to be "a little con artist," as she later put it, Beverly pulled the same stunt with sleds and Mickey Mouse watches. "I was shameless," she admitted cheerfully.

Bowes, who recognized Beverly's talent, suggested she begin professional voice lessons. Following his recommendation, Shirley Silverman made an appointment with Estelle Liebling, one of New York's most highly respected singing teachers. When Beverly and her

Operators take listeners' calls during a broadcast of the "Major Bowes' Original Amateur Hour." Calls from enthusiastic fans flooded the show's switchboards after each performance.

mother arrived at Liebling's studio, the youngster was told to wait in the reception area while her mother sang. Informed that Beverly was the candidate for lessons, Liebling could hardly believe her ears. "I don't teach little girls," Sills recalled her saying. "I don't even *know* any little girls."

But Shirley Silverman persuaded her to listen to Beverly, who proceeded to sing an Italian aria she had heard on her mother's record player. When Beverly finished the aria, Liebling just laughed, prompting the youngster to burst into

Voice teacher Estelle Liebling (above) accepted Sills as a student in 1936. She would be Sills's vocal mentor until her death in 1970.

tears. Apologizing for her laughter, Liebling explained that Beverly had just sung an imitation of an Amelita Galli-Curci aria that Liebling herself had taught the great soprano. She acknowledged, however, that the 7-year-old applicant had talent and agreed to give her a 15-minute lesson every Saturday morning.

Because opera requires more than vocal technique, Liebling advised Beverly to take piano lessons as well as instruction in Italian and French. She

particularly wanted the youngster to understand Italian so she would know the meaning of the words she sang instead of merely mimicking them. Liebling also demanded that Beverly, who tended to fidget when she sang, stand still. During Beverly's first lesson, Liebling told her that she must not move from a medallion that was woven into the center of the large Oriental rug that covered the studio floor. "That," recalled Sills, "was the first discipline I ever learned as a singer."

Beverly learned to stand still. She also learned to spend hours each day singing the endless scales and tedious vocal exercises her teacher assigned. Until then, singing had been something the youngster did for fun, always enjoying the praise and attention she earned. She was just beginning to realize how much hard work an operatic career would require.

Although Beverly had sung arias on national radio, she had never seen an opera. When she was eight years old, a year after she started studying with Liebling, her mother took her to an afternoon performance at the Metropolitan Opera, then as now considered America's leading opera company. At this time, the Met, which would later move uptown, was on Broadway and 39th Street. The first sight of the huge Met stage, with its golden curtain and elaborately carved proscenium arch, was an awesome experience even for an adult; for an eight year old, it was overwhelming. That visit to the opera determined the future course of Beverly Sills's life.

The opera presented at the Met that day was *Lakmé*; the soprano singing the title role was Beverly's idol, Lily Pons. When the curtain rose on the first act, Beverly saw a set depicting the exotic temples and palm trees of India. She realized then that arias were just part of the total operatic experience.

Fifty years later, the thrill of that occasion was still vivid to her. "I really got hooked by that performance," she told an interviewer. "Until then, I loved singing arias and the fact that everybody paid attention to me when I did. I just thought that an opera singer is a lady who sings all those high notes

Soprano Geraldine Farrar performs at the Metropolitan Opera House in 1906. Thirty years later, Sills was stunned by her first sight of the magnificent theater.

and those special songs. But I didn't actually know that arias were from operas. When my mother took me to see *Lakmé* at the Metropolitan, I realized that there was a whole story here, that there was much more to opera than arias, wonderful as they were.

"At the Met, I saw the costumes and the scenery and the dancing and heard the sound of that orchestra. And then this exquisite tiny creature walked out onstage. It was Lily Pons. I decided then and there that I was going to be just like her. I was so excited to see all that went on in opera, and I decided that I just had to participate in it. I went home that night and kept telling my father that I was going to be an opera star just like Lily Pons. I just got absolutely nuts for the art."

At her next voice lesson, Beverly asked Estelle Liebling to teach her more of the arias Lily Pons sang. Because those high, light arias suited Sills's voice well, Liebling agreed. Beverly was thrilled. She could not know then that years later she would be famous for singing such arias. Nor could she know that she would bring a dramatic dimension to her operatic roles that Pons herself never possessed.

From the outset of her career, Beverly Sills had demonstrated an instinct for drama as well as for music. When she was 11, after appearing as a regular guest on "Capitol Family" for 4 years, she got a job as a radio actress. For the next year, she played a mistreated child opera singer in "Our Gal Sunday," one of the nation's most popular soap operas. Heard on one of these "soaps"—so

called because they were usually sponsored by cleaning-product companies— was radio's first singing commercial: a female voice chirping, "Rinso white, Rinso bright, happy little washday song!" The singer was Beverly Sills, who had received the historic assignment on the recommendation of her friend Major Bowes. Recordings of that commercial are now in the collections of several radio museums.

When Beverly was 12 years old, her father insisted that she end her radio career and concentrate on her academic studies. Although she was doing well in school, Morris Silverman wanted her to have what he regarded as a more normal life. In spite of her father's sometimes stern ways—"Papa had always been a bear," said his daughter— Beverly had always had a warm and loving relationship with him, and she obeyed his wishes. Her radio appearances stopped.

Like her schoolmates, Beverly played tennis, went swimming, and rooted for the Brooklyn Dodgers, but while her friends socialized and participated in extracurricular activities, she took lessons in voice and piano, studied foreign languages, and went to the opera as often as possible. Estelle Liebling now taught her for an hour each week. Through years of vocal exercises, which Liebling carefully tailored for Sills's young voice, the soprano had developed a strong vocal technique based on absolute control of her breath. She had begun to learn more than arias; she studied entire operas. By the age of 15, she knew 20 complete roles.

And by that age, Beverly had also acquired her first steady boyfriend. Sandy Levine, she recalled in her autobiography, "was a good-looking blond boy and an excellent athlete." Although the two spent as much time together as they could, they were seldom alone with each other. "As was the style then," Sills later noted, "we traveled in groups that went bowling . . . or to the movies or to the Sweet Shoppe . . . or to somebody's house where we played records and danced." The relationship was innocent, but Morris Silverman never quite approved of his daughter's boyfriend. Instead of ringing the doorbell when he called for her, Sandy usually stood outside, whistling Beverly's "Rinso white, Rinso bright" commercial. "Are you going out with a boy or a bird?" asked an irritated Morris Silverman.

Also at the age of 15, Beverly resumed her performing career. Deciding her student was ready to be heard professionally, Liebling arranged an audition for her with J. J. Shubert, a powerful Broadway producer who owned a string of theaters across the country. Impressed by Sills's voice, Shubert offered her a contract to go on tour with a new repertory company he had assembled. The company would present seven operettas written by W. S. Gilbert and Sir Arthur Sullivan, the 19th-century British librettist-composer team responsible for such works as *The Mikado* and *The Pirates of Penzance*. Like operas, operettas are a form of musical theater, but they do not demand the highly developed vocal

An 1881 cartoon depicts librettist W. S. Gilbert (left) and composer Arthur Sullivan, the British team responsible for such popular operettas as The Mikado.

technique of the operatic stage. At 15, Sills was young to be a member of the Gilbert and Sullivan troupe, but her singing voice made her the equal of the company's other members, and her height (5 feet, 8½ inches) and weight (130 pounds) made her look older than she was.

Morris Silverman did not consider show business a proper environment for a 15-year-old girl. He was appalled by the idea of his daughter on tour. He was glad Beverly was multilingual and that she read voraciously, but he wanted her to have a traditional life. In the 1940s, middle-class girls were expected to grow up "cultured," exposed to a smattering of the arts and possibly a college education, but careers were not a priority. They might work temporarily as teachers or nurses, but they would then "settle down" as wives and mothers.

Beverly's mother, who had nurtured her daughter's talent and who regarded the Shubert tour as a good opportunity for her to acquire onstage experience, intervened. Defying her husband, she signed Beverly's contract with Shubert.

Beverly had been attending the Professional Children's School in Manhattan and arranged to keep up with her schoolwork by correspondence while she was on tour. Being away from home was a new experience for her; except for one summer at camp, she had never been separated from her family. But during the next two months, this native New Yorker found herself singing in Providence, Boston, Hartford, Montreal, Toronto, Detroit, Cleveland, Madison, Milwaukee, Grand Rapids, Indianapolis, and Cincinnati. The troupe stayed from three to six days in each city, performing every night.

The tour taught Sills what it was like to go onstage and sing after spending the whole day traveling; it also taught her how to hold down expenses on the road. She often dined in her small hotel room, eating a can of stew warmed on a hot plate, with peanut brittle as a side dish. A trouper's life had its difficult moments, but to Sills, singing before an audience day after day was a joy. She had never known stage fright and never would. Performing was always second nature to her.

Returning from the tour, Sills was surprised to learn that her boyfriend, Sandy Levine, had started to date someone else. But the breakup of her first romance left her calm: "I came back to Brooklyn," she recalled, "a much worldlier young woman than when I'd left it." Her career was now the focus of her life. On the tour, Beverly had completed her correspondence course, and in June 1944, she received her high school diploma. In September, she left for a second Shubert-sponsored tour, this time playing the leads in two Viennese operettas, *The Merry Widow* and *Countess Maritza*.

When Beverly got home in December, her father put his foot down. (And Morris Silverman, noted his daughter, "had a heavy foot.") She could, he said, go to college—his first choice for her—or she could stay home and study full-time for a serious operatic career. In either case, there would be no more operetta tours. This time, her mother concurred.

Shirley Silverman realized that Beverly had nothing to gain by neglecting her voice lessons for the months of yet another tour. The operettas had given her stage experience; now, if she elected to commit herself to opera, she needed more solid training and, eventually, appearances in opera. Faced with the choice of further academic studies or pursuit of an operatic career, Beverly Sills decided without hesitation. Her choice, of course, was opera.

She began a period of intensive study, working both with Estelle Liebling and with Giuseppe Bamboschek, artistic director of the Philadelphia Opera Company. Bamboschek, a close friend of Liebling's, allowed Sills to understudy the stars of several Philadelphia productions, and in February 1947, he cast her in a small role. She made her operatic debut as the gypsy girl Frasquita, in French composer Georges Bizet's (1838–75) *Carmen*. "I was now an opera singer," she observed in her autobiography. "I knew great things were about to open up for me. It's funny how dumb you can be at 17, isn't it?"

Beverly Sills chose to pursue serious operatic training rather than attend college. She took voice lessons in New York and Paris and held down a variety of singing jobs.

T H R E E

On the Road

When Sills won a role in *Carmen*, she thought her career as a *diva* (an opera star) had begun. But success was not to come so quickly. To the surprise of 17-year-old Sills, who expected instant stardom, her 1947 appearance in *Carmen* opened no new doors for her: As she wryly noted in her autobiography, "Seventeen-year-old divas are rare." Through Estelle Liebling, she did find several opportunities to sing: She made a two-week concert tour of the Midwest with five other young musicians and performed in a series of concerts at New England colleges with a choral group. She enjoyed the performances, but, she asked herself, "what the hell did it have to do with being an opera singer?"

Because the sporadic concerts brought in little money, Sills continued to rely on her parents for financial support. In late 1948, however, life at home changed radically. Morris Silverman was suddenly taken seriously ill.

At first his symptoms were diagnosed as tuberculosis, but tests eventually showed that he had lung cancer. Silverman—who had smoked three packs of cigarettes a day all his adult life—was dying, but neither he nor his wife revealed the truth to their children. While Sills and her brothers were spared the agony of this knowledge, they were also denied the chance to prepare themselves for his death. Silverman was scheduled to undergo a series of operations in August 1949. That same month, his daughter was offered a job: singing for the passengers of a cruise ship during a month-long trip to South America. Her parents urged her to go, insisting that her father's recovery from the impending surgery was certain. When Sills returned from three glamorous weeks aboard ship, her mother was waiting at the pier, dressed in black. Morris Silverman had died five days earlier.

Sills was shattered. Silverman had

The Grand Staircase of the Paris Opera dominates the interior of the magnificent landmark, completed in 1874. Sills studied voice there in 1950.

been a protective, caring father who had been the basis of her sense of stability and security. He had also been the primary source of strength for the whole family. "My father had always taken care of *everything*," Sills later recalled. Now his wife and children had to find strength within themselves.

With Sidney and Stanley Silverman away at college, Sills and her mother needed less space, so they moved into a small one-bedroom apartment. Shirley Silverman, who had always been an excellent seamstress, learned to be a hat designer, and Sills took a singing job at a private Manhattan nightclub. Again, her work had nothing to do with opera, but it provided a good, steady income.

During the day, Sills continued her lessons with Liebling, always following up at home with preparation for the next lesson. By 1950, she had saved enough money to take herself and her mother to France, where the soprano participated in a summer workshop at the Paris Opera. (Opera originated in Italy, then spread to France, Germany, and Austria; the traditional style of operatic singing and performing is taught in these four countries.) The Paris workshop gave Sills the chance to perfect her French pronunciation and to learn more about the French style of performing, which tends to be delicate and introspective. Among the operas Sills studied in Paris that summer was one by French composer Jules Massenet (1842–1912): *Manon*, a work in which she was later to become world renowned.

While studying in Paris, Sills took in the local sights, including the Eiffel Tower. She enjoyed her stay but was eager to return to the United States.

Sills relished the opportunity to be in Paris. She climbed the Eiffel Tower, visited the celebrated Louvre museum, and roamed the historic streets and squares. But she had no intention of staying on, as many other young American singers did. Because most opera stars of the time were European, many Americans tried to launch their careers with small European opera companies in order to return to the United States as established operatic singers. Sills, however, was determined to succeed in her native land. When the workshop ended, she and her mother returned to New York.

At 21, Sills had been an opera student for 14 years; by now she was more than eager to perform. She told Liebling that she wanted to audition for the Metropolitan Opera. Her teacher knew that the young soprano was not prepared for this giant step in her career. Nevertheless, Liebling arranged an audition for her with Désiré Defrére, a stage director at the Met. Defrére was about to direct a series of operas for the Wagner Opera's touring company, an organization that presented operas in auditoriums and high school gymnasiums around the country. As soon as he heard Sills sing, the director signed her up for the company's 1951 tour. "That tour," noted the soprano in her autobiography, "began my operatic career."

The routine was grueling, involving long daily bus trips, hastily gobbled meals, and little sleep. Sills was familiar with life on the road from her days with the Shubert troupe, but there the pace had been less hectic and the stops longer than overnight. And Gilbert and Sullivan operettas were far less taxing than full-scale operas.

On this tour, Sills sang the part of Violetta in Verdi's *La Traviata*, one of the most demanding roles in the soprano repertoire. Violetta, a beautiful Parisienne, lives a frenetic, pleasure-seeking life even though she knows she is terminally ill with tuberculosis. Then she falls in love with Alfredo and moves with him to the country, where she is very happy. But because her former way of life brings shame on Alfredo's family, Violetta decides to leave him, sacrificing the only real joy she has ever known. At the end, the lovers are reunited, and she dies in his arms.

Sills worked on her interpretation of the role with Defrére. He showed her the fine points of stage makeup and taught her to walk and even think like the character she was portraying. In order to deepen her interpretation of Violetta, who is based on a real 19th-century woman, Defrére encouraged Sills to read as much as possible about her. After each performance, the director reviewed her work, and Sills made those changes they agreed on, improving her characterization with each performance.

The music Verdi wrote for Violetta ranges from an exuberant drinking song in the first act to a final, achingly beautiful aria in which she bids farewell to the past. The soprano who plays Violetta needs a combination of musical ability and dramatic talent. In addition to singing this difficult music for almost three hours, she must be able to communicate to the audience Violetta's transformation from flippant courtesan to tragic heroine. Most sopranos require several days of rest before and after singing Violetta. On the Wagner expedition, Sills sang the role 54 times in 9 weeks. "When I finished the tour," she wrote later, "I could sing Violetta standing on my head or doing somersaults."

After the tour, Sills made a few con-

In 1951, Sills made her debut as Violetta, the heroine of Verdi's 1853 opera, La Traviata. The soprano sang the taxing role 54 times in 9 weeks.

After her father's death, Sills worked to help her mother make ends meet. She sang at the Concord Hotel (shown) in upstate New York during the summer of 1952.

caela, the hero's country sweetheart, in *Carmen*. Micaela was not among Sills's favorite roles; she called it "limited, frustrating, and a bore." But the job paid well—$100 per performance—and she spent her offstage time teaching herself to play the guitar and reading every book she could lay her hands on.

In the fall of 1953, Sills spent three months singing minor roles with the San Francisco Opera, an important company whose roster included many international stars. In San Francisco, Sills had the chance to watch experienced singers at work and to see how they solved dramatic and vocal problems. She learned not only by observing but by making her own mistakes; it was there that she forgot to check her Valkyrie helmet for size.

Recounting the helmet episode afterward, Sills treated it as a joke. But at the time, she said in her autobiography, "it was no laughing matter." When the fallen headpiece rolled to the front of the stage, she scrambled after it, much to the hilarity of the audience—and the fury of the opera's director, Kurt Adler. He confronted her after the final curtain: "Sills, are you drunk?" he bellowed. "You could take the girl out of Brooklyn," she later observed, "but you couldn't take Brooklyn out of the girl. I told Adler to drop dead." Sills paid for her retort. She was not asked to return to the San Francisco Opera for 18 years. Eventually, she and Adler made up and became good friends.

Sills received several good notices for her work in San Francisco, but she longed to make her New York debut. In

cert appearances. Then, in the summer of 1952, she took a one-day-a-week job at the Concord Hotel, a resort in New York State's Catskill Mountains popular with Jewish vacationers. She recalled the experience fondly. The hotel's "huge rooms were packed with appreciative Jews," she said, "the food was fantastic, and I got to sing a lot of my high notes—not a bad way to spend an evening."

The following fall, Sills signed up for another road trip with the Wagner company. This time she was cast as Mi-

A prop keeper stores helmets at the Metropolitan Opera House. Sills accidentally created a sensation when she lost her helmet during a 1953 performance.

December 1953, she decided to audition for the New York City Opera, founded in 1944 as the city's resident opera company. Unlike the Met, which presented operas from September through April, City Opera staged performances for one month in the spring and one in the fall. The Met was celebrated for its spectacular productions and a roster of international stars; City Opera's sets and costumes were more modest, and it kept its ticket prices low. The company was made up of young performers, most of them American, who sang and acted together as an ensemble company. Their performances were held in the cavernous auditorium known as the City Center of Music and Drama.

Because Sills had been so successful with *La Traviata* on tour, she sang Violetta's first-act aria as an audition piece for City Opera's general director, Dr. Joseph Rosenstock. When she finished, his only words were "Thank you." Six more auditions followed; nothing happened. Sills, now an experienced opera singer who knew she could handle a role both vocally and dramatically, was mystified. Then, through her agent, she learned that Rosenstock thought she had a "phenomenal voice but no personality." The news of his reaction would have been laughable if it had not been such an obstacle to her career.

"I nearly exploded," recalled the ebullient, loquacious singer. In her au-

Still in use as a theater and lecture hall, New York City Center (below) served as City Opera's home from 1944 until its move to Lincoln Center in 1968.

tobiography, she recounted her reaction to Rosenstock's words: "No personality? Fine. Throughout all those auditions . . . I'd always dressed in very subdued clothing. Well, forget that. I'd worn jumpers and high-necked blouses to the previous auditions. The eighth time out, I showed up in a jumper—but without a blouse underneath. I bought myself a pair of black mesh stockings and the highest heels I could find. I'd always tied my hair back in a bun; this time I let it hang all the way down my back."

Sills not only looked dramatic, she sounded dramatic. The aria she sang was not one of her favorites (she had used all of them in her earlier tryouts), but she showed Rosenstock that Beverly Sills was anything but bland. "I was *very* angry," she recalled, "and believe me, he knew it." After the audition, Rosenstock said, "Okay, Sills. Upstairs to my office, you've got yourself a job." He presented her with a contract to sing a performance of Rosalinda, one of two leading roles in the comic Viennese work *Die Fledermaus* (The Bat). She would also understudy two other roles that season. "It had been a long haul," Sills wrote later, "and I was not so much elated as relieved."

Beverly Sills made her City Opera debut in *Fledermaus* on October 29, 1955. The audience was enthusiastic, but no one applauded as vigorously as the corsage-wearing woman near the front of the orchestra. Shirley Silverman beamed as soprano Beverly Sills took her curtain calls. The next day,

Sills appears as Rosalinda in Die Fledermaus, *the work in which she made her 1955 New York City Opera debut. She landed the role after eight auditions.*

the *New York Times* declared that in Sills the company had added "an accomplished singing actress to its roster." Although her debut did not make Sills a star, it established her as a City Opera regular.

Sills's first experience as a City Opera understudy was less auspicious. The opera was *The Golden Slippers*, a rarely performed work by Russian composer Pyotr Tchaikovsky (1840–93). When the scheduled soprano failed to show up for a performance, understudy Sills had less than an hour's rehearsal time onstage. Nevertheless, all went well until the final scene, when the hero brings the soprano a pair of golden slippers. She is supposed to put them on and dance with her lover as the curtain comes down on the predictably happy ending.

In her hurry to prepare for the performance, Sills had neglected to try on the slippers, designed for the soprano she was replacing. At the appropriate moment, the hero ceremoniously placed the golden shoes at her feet. She slipped into them, and, as she began to dance, out of them. (Sills later called the incident "a case of the helmet revisited.") She left the empty slippers in the middle of the stage and danced barefoot until the curtain came down. The audience was laughing, and so was Sills. But Rosenstock, she noted, "was not amused."

Despite his anger about the slipper incident, Rosenstock invited Sills to sing during the spring season and to join the company on its month-long tour following the New York perfor-

Sills met Peter Greenough (pictured) while performing in Cleveland, Ohio. When she returned to New York, she told her mother she had found the man she meant to marry.

mances. The tour ended in Cleveland, Ohio, where the company was invited to a reception by the local press club.

Exhausted by her travels, Sills wanted to relax at a movie instead of going to the reception, but City Opera officials insisted, and she dutifully complied. Seated at her table was Peter Greenough, associate editor of the *Cleveland Plain Dealer*, a newspaper owned by his family. He was tall, handsome, and obviously intrigued by the redheaded soprano with dimples and a creamy complexion. Greenough scribbled a note on a matchbook, asking to see her. She agreed to have dinner with him the following night.

When Greenough called for Sills at her hotel, he was accompanied by two little girls: his daughters Lindley, nine, and Nancy, six. Sills asked where their mother was. "Right at the moment," said Greenough, "I don't know." The foursome climbed into Greenough's station wagon and headed home for dinner. As they drove, Sills later recalled in her autobiography, she was thinking, "Who is this guy, anyway, what is this with his kids, he doesn't even know where his wife is, and this is the dumbest move I have ever made."

Home turned out to be a 25-room mansion on Lake Erie. Two maids served dinner, then took the girls upstairs to bed. Escorting Sills into the elegant living room, Greenough tried to create a romantic atmosphere by lighting a fire. But he forgot to open the flue, and smoke soon filled the room, forcing the couple to take refuge in the kitchen.

There they talked for hours. Sills told Greenough about her life in New York and about her dreams. He told her he had grown up near Boston, graduated from Harvard, and received a master's degree in journalism from Columbia University. A direct descendant of John Alden, who had arrived in America aboard the *Mayflower* in 1620, Greenough had seen action in Europe during World War II and afterward had

become a newspaper reporter. He said that his wife was an alcoholic and had left him for another man and that he was in the process of divorcing her and trying to gain custody of the girls. His third and youngest daughter, Diana, was retarded and away at a special school.

The next morning, Greenough drove Sills from her hotel to the airport for her flight back to New York. The soprano had dated a great deal since high school, but she had never been serious about anyone. When she got home, not even 48 hours after she met Peter Greenough, she told her mother that she had met the man she wanted to marry. Shirley Silverman was delighted until Sills told her that Greenough was married, had 3 children, was 12 years older than she was, and was not Jewish. Her mother burst into tears and, Sills later reported, wailed, "Why does everything have to happen to my baby?"

But when Shirley Silverman met Greenough, she was won over by his charm. He soon proposed to Sills, who, with her mother's approval, happily accepted. On November 17, 1956, six weeks after Greenough's divorce came through, he and Sills were married. The ceremony took place in Estelle Liebling's studio. When the couple took their vows, they stood on the medallion in the center of the Oriental rug—the exact spot where Beverly Sills had stood still for her singing lessons 20 years earlier.

Sills sings the title role in Douglas Moore's 1956 opera, The Ballad of Baby Doe. *After the soprano's audition, Moore said, "Miss Sills, you are* Baby Doe."

FOUR

From Triumph to Tragedy

After a honeymoon in Nassau, the Bahamas, Sills and Greenough returned to Cleveland. There, pasted on the door of their lakefront home, they found a message from Lindley and Nancy: "Welcome home, Mama and Daddy!" To the 27-year-old Sills, the words promised a smooth beginning to her new marriage. Her relationship with her husband was everything she had hoped for, but Sills soon found that getting along with his daughters was another matter. Caught in a custody battle between their parents, the girls began to blame Sills for the divorce. Her efforts to introduce any rules were met with resistance, even defiance. She, in turn, hesitated to discipline the girls when they misbehaved.

Adding to Sills's problems, her once-close Brooklyn relatives now shunned her because she had married outside the Jewish religion. On the other side of the coin, many of her husband's socially prominent acquaintances snubbed her *because* she was Jewish. Greenough family members sometimes invited the newlyweds to their homes, but only for large, formal gatherings. At one point, Sills decided to host a party for an old friend, a conductor visiting Cleveland on a Metropolitan Opera tour. She bought flowers, hired musicians and caterers, and sent invitations to 40 people. Most of them accepted, but on the evening of the party, only one couple showed up.

Sills gradually came to terms with her role as stepmother. And in the long run, Sills's extended family reconciled itself to her marriage to Greenough. But Cleveland society never accepted Sills, and Sills, who missed New York deeply, never accepted Cleveland as her home. In the fall of 1957, when Julius Rudel, the new manager of the New York City Opera, asked her to sing Violetta in *La Traviata*, she accepted with delight. With her performances of *La Traviata* that season, the press began to notice that Beverly Sills was more than just a competent, reliable singer. Real recognition, however, came the following year.

Rudel announced that City Opera's 1958 spring season would be entirely devoted to contemporary American opera. It was a bold plan: The popular operas, those guaranteed to draw audiences, are Italian, French, or German. American opera was largely unknown.

When Rudel proclaimed the special season, the work that generated the most interest among New York opera fans was *The Ballad of Baby Doe*. Composed by Pulitzer Prize winner Douglas Moore, the opera had been performed for the first time two years earlier in Central City, Colorado. City Opera scheduled its New York premiere for April 3, 1958.

Baby Doe is based on the romance between two historical characters out of the Old West: Horace Tabor, a

When she married Peter Greenough, Sills moved to Cleveland (shown) to live with him. Her husband's family snubbed her, though, and she never considered Cleveland her home.

Composer Douglas Moore (above) used American themes for most of his operas. They include The Ballad of Baby Doe, Carry Nation, *and* The Devil and Daniel Webster.

The character Sills played in The Ballad of Baby Doe *was based on real-life figure Elizabeth McCourt (pictured), who kept vigil for her dead lover for more than 30 years.*

wealthy silver-mine owner in 19th-century Colorado, and the beautiful Elizabeth McCourt, known as Baby Doe, who left her husband for Tabor. At his death in 1899, Tabor, by then bankrupt, asked Baby Doe to guard the silver mine that had produced his fortune. More than 30 years later, she was found at the abandoned mine, frozen to death.

Sills had expressed interest in performing the title role, but conductor Emerson Buckley told her she was too tall to play Baby Doe, whom the com-

poser describes as "a fluffy kitten." Self-conscious about her height since her teens, the tall, broad-shouldered soprano dismissed the thought of trying out for the part.

In early February, Julius Rudel telephoned Sills, begging her to audition for *Baby Doe*. The composer and the conductor, he said, had auditioned more than 100 sopranos for the role, and not one had met with their approval. With less than two months before the premiere, City Opera was in a state of panic. Sills refused to audition.

Rudel sent Sills copies of two soprano arias from the opera; she found them beautiful and compelling, but her answer was still no. Then her husband entered the battle, insisting that he wanted to celebrate his birthday at a Broadway show. Why not, he asked, audition for Moore while they were in New York? Sills saw through his flimsy plot, but she decided to go along with it. She would do the audition, but on her own terms.

She arrived at the City Center audition wearing spike-heeled shoes, a suit, and a towering white-mink hat. "When I walked onstage," she recalled, "I must have stood about six feet five." As Sills told the story in *Beverly*, she stalked to the center of the stage, looked at composer Moore, and announced, "This is how big I am before I sing, and I'm going to be just as big when I finish. So if I'm too big for your Baby Doe, you can save my energy and your time by saying so right now." Moore, a gentle and courteous man, simply answered: "Oh, Miss Sills, you look just fine to me."

Sills sang the opera's "Willow Song" aria. When she finished, an awed Moore said softly: "Miss Sills, you *are* Baby Doe." Near pandemonium ruled the next few weeks. Sills had to learn the role quickly, and because the title role was cast so late, rehearsal time was shorter than usual. Nevertheless, the opening of *Baby Doe* provided Sills with her first major triumph. The first person she pleased was herself: "Everything I did worked perfectly," she said later. "I'd never experienced anything approaching that feeling before." The press agreed with her self-appraisal. The *New York Times* notice contained high praise for *Baby Doe* and its star; the New York *Herald Tribune* ran a rave review on page one.

Still glowing with pride about *Baby Doe*, Sills returned to Cleveland after the opera's three scheduled performances. Before the year was out, she had another cause for rejoicing: In late December she and her husband, who had been hoping for a baby of their own, discovered she was pregnant. While she awaited the birth of her baby, Sills kept working. In the spring of 1959, she once again sang *Baby Doe* with City Opera, where she also appeared in a new opera, *Six Characters in Search of an Author*. Unlike *Baby Doe*, *Six Characters* failed to please a single critic. The *New York Daily News*, for example, headlined its review "Six Characters in Search of a Composer." But Sills, six months pregnant, was singled out as a bright spot in an otherwise dreary production.

In June, Sills returned to New York to record the cast album of *The Ballad of Baby Doe*. "I was so large by then," she recalled with amusement, "that I had to argue my way on board our flight from New York to Cleveland." A few weeks later, on August 4, 1959, she gave birth to Meredith Holden Greenough. The baby girl, who would be known as Muffy, spent a harrowing first week of life: Born with both yellow jaundice and a serious respiratory disorder, she developed a 105-degree fever and breathed with difficulty. But

The Ballad of Baby Doe *received rave reviews from opera critics and added to Sills's growing professional reputation. Sills and the rest of the cast recorded the opera on an album.*

after eight days in an incubator and a series of drug injections, Muffy was well on the road to recovery, and Beverly Sills Greenough took her eight-day-old daughter home.

Sills loved being with her baby; she no longer felt torn between home and career. She canceled her fall appearances at City Opera and agreed to do only three performances the following spring. A proud Shirley Silverman, laden with hand-sewn baby clothes, often visited her new grandchild, who also delighted Sills's stepdaughters.

Sills did not reappear at City Opera until the spring of 1962. She put her career on hold not only for Muffy but

for her husband, who, in 1960, found himself in a bitter family struggle over the management of the *Cleveland Plain Dealer*. The battle ended with the sale of the newspaper. When the *Boston Globe* offered him a job as a financial columnist, he and his wife, who was expecting her second child, decided to move east.

The family settled into a handsome 19-room house in the Boston suburb of Milton. The move elated Sills: Boston had just acquired its own opera company, and she was now only an hour's flight from New York. On June 29, 1961, several months after her arrival in Milton, Sills gave birth to a son, Peter Bulkeley Greenough, Jr. Bucky, as he was called by his family, was a big baby with none of the problems at birth that had threatened Muffy's life.

Twenty-two months old when her brother was born, Muffy was a beautiful, intelligent, and well-coordinated toddler, but she had not yet learned to speak. Her parents had begun to suspect that the little girl had a hearing problem, and two months after Bucky's birth, their fears were confirmed: "Your daughter," said the specialist they consulted, "has a profound loss of hearing." The doctor assured the stricken parents that Muffy was highly intelligent and had no learning problems, but the news of her deafness was devastating.

Sills could not know then that Muffy would develop into an independent, productive human being. Ironically, however, the daughter of the woman who delighted audiences with her sing-

After she and her family moved to Boston, Sills gave birth to her second child, a son nicknamed "Bucky." At Boston's Children's Hospital (above), she learned Bucky was retarded.

husband took Muffy to be fitted with a hearing aid; although the youngster would never be able to hear normally, the device helped her identify sounds by their frequencies. Muffy's parents arranged for special lessons for their daughter, and they began to learn everything they could about solving the problems of the deaf.

Soon after she learned about her daughter's deafness, Sills began to worry about her son, who often experienced moments when his eyes crossed sharply and his hands seemed out of control. Could he, she wondered, have "some sort of nerve affliction?" When she took him to Children's Hospital in Boston, she received shocking news: Bucky was hopelessly retarded. He would never talk, never develop normally. Within six weeks, Sills and her husband had learned that both their children faced an uncertain future.

Talking to an interviewer years later, Sills said, "It took me a long time to get back, to get it all together mentally, emotionally, vocally." In the meantime, she devoted almost all her time to her children. She hired a young woman to help her care for Bucky; the two watched him constantly, especially as he grew older, to prevent him from hurting himself. And every day, she took Muffy to a Boston nursery school that specialized in training deaf children. There, she and a speech therapist spent hours trying to teach Muffy to read lips and encouraging her to blow out candles so she would learn how to make the "wh" sound. "Even the most tedious lessons never

ing would never hear the sound of her mother's voice. But that thought was far from the soprano's mind then. "I was a mother whose gorgeous daughter was deaf," she wrote later. "My voice was the last thing I worried about Muffy's not being able to hear."

Aching for her little girl, Sills managed to pull herself together and do what she had to do. First, she and her seemed to tire her," Sills wrote later. "What pulled us all through was the unfailing cheerfulness of my baby girl. She never stopped smiling, never stopped laughing."

Before her children's diagnoses, Sills had been flying to New York once a week to see her mother and take lessons with Estelle Liebling. After she learned of her children's problems, she canceled her lessons, quit going to New York, and rarely left her house. "I had no desire to sing," she said later. "I just couldn't."

Eleven months after Bucky's birth, Peter Greenough decided his wife simply had to get out of the house and return to her singing. On May 26, 1962, her 33rd birthday, he gave her a present: Fifty-two round-trip tickets between Boston and New York, a year's supply. As she wrote later, "He wanted me to resume my weekly lessons with Miss Liebling, to start seeing my mother in New York, to get back into opera again—and to stop feeling sorry for the kids and for myself." Eventually, Greenough got what he wanted.

Beverly Sills and her daughter, Muffy Greenough, play a spirited game of softball at their summer home in Martha's Vineyard, Massachusetts.

FIVE

Prima Donna

When Peter gave me those round-trip tickets, I was forced to go into New York," recalled Sills. "I had my singing teacher there, and eventually, it all came back."

For any opera singer, performing after even a short vacation requires a period of adjustment and retraining. For Sills, who had not sung for nearly a year, getting her vocal cords into condition and regaining her breath control involved several months of constant effort. Even when she was back in shape vocally, the hard work continued. It always does for an opera singer; the career demands ongoing self-discipline. Throughout her years onstage, Sills vocalized every day, continued working on languages, watched her diet carefully, avoided smoky rooms, and made sure she got enough rest.

"One of the most difficult disciplines to acquire is that of self-appraisal, real self-appraisal, to be your own worst and best critic," said Sills in a 1988 interview. "I used to take a yellow marker and mark on the score where I couldn't accomplish what I wanted to do during a performance or a lesson—maybe sing a whole phrase in one breath, maybe sing a high note very softly. I would underline it and work on it the next day.

"Once I was able to accomplish what I wanted, a red line went over it. That way, if I got a wonderful reception from the public and the press, but I knew I had not done what I set out to do, I never let it sway me. I still went and fixed that part that I didn't like. On the other hand, if I came back and said 'There, I did it,' and I read in the newspaper the next day that I hadn't, it never bothered me as much. It bothered me because everybody likes praise; but I had my yellow crayon and I knew what I was doing.

"If you know it's good, nobody and

Singing the Queen of the Night in Mozart's opera The Magic Flute, *Sills hits a high F. Although she excelled as the Queen, the soprano detested the role.*

nothing can take it away from you. And if you know it's bad, nothing can convince you that it was good, not all the praise in the world. This discipline of self-appraisal really even goes for people off the stage; this idea of knowing your own worth, even if other people don't appear to recognize it. If inside you know your own value, you won't succumb to peer pressure. It takes a great deal of courage to be yourself."

Beverly Sills went back to singing at the New York City Opera on a regular basis. She also performed in Boston, Philadelphia, Honolulu, New Orleans, Cincinnati, and Fort Lauderdale. In 1964, Boston conductor Sarah Caldwell asked her to sing the Queen of the Night in Wolfgang Amadeus Mozart's *Magic Flute*. It was not a role that pleased the soprano; she called it "boring and pointless." But she accepted, largely because the part is extremely difficult to sing. Sills always found it hard to resist a challenge.

The role of Queen of the Night consists almost entirely of two arias, which contain five high F's. "How high is a high F?" asked Sills in her autobiography. "*Very* high. In addition to those five high F's, the Queen's two arias contain some rather difficult coloratura passages. And you can't be a pipsqueak soprano. . . . You've really got to be able to sock those notes out there." Sills socked those notes, delighting her Boston audience and bringing her an invitation to do it again, this time at Switzerland's Mozart Festival.

Sills scored a triumph at the festival. Because so few sopranos are able to sing the Queen's role, she was asked to perform it repeatedly in the years that followed. But she never enjoyed it and sang it only until she felt solidly established in her profession. "The minute I was in a position to say goodbye to *The Magic Flute*," she wrote later, "I did."

Sills went on to play Olympia, a mechanical doll in *The Tales of Hoffmann*; Constanza in Mozart's *The Abduction from the Seraglio*; and the fragile Mimi in Puccini's *La Bohème*;

Sills plays a doll in The Tales of Hoffmann, *a 19th-century opera composed by Jacques Offenbach and based on stories by German writer-composer E. T. A. Hoffmann.*

among other roles. One performance that stuck in her mind took place in Cincinnati, Ohio. She sang Violetta at the Cincinnati Zoo Opera, so called because its open-sided theater stood in the middle of the city zoo. On this occasion, the soprano's principal aria was all but drowned out by the barking of sea lions; the opera, she said, "should have been billed 'Starring Beverly Seals.'"

Sills's reputation in the United States was growing. She still spent most of her working hours at her "second home," the New York City Opera. Between 1962 and 1966, she performed an extraordinary range of roles—roles that required dramatic versatility as well as highly polished vocal technique.

During these years, the conflict between Sills's personal and professional lives intensified. She got home as often as she could—usually after each City Opera performance—but she always seemed to be either arriving or departing. Looking back on this period of her life in 1988, Sills said, "I don't know where all the energy came from. It's a great problem, especially for a woman. Men seem to feel it less. As long as Mama's home, everybody seems to feel secure. They were very difficult times. There's no doubt about that."

Professionally, Sills knew her own worth. She had become a drawing card

Patrons take their seats at the open-air Cincinnati Zoo Opera. Sill's 1962 performance there was punctuated by a serenade from a chorus of sea lions.

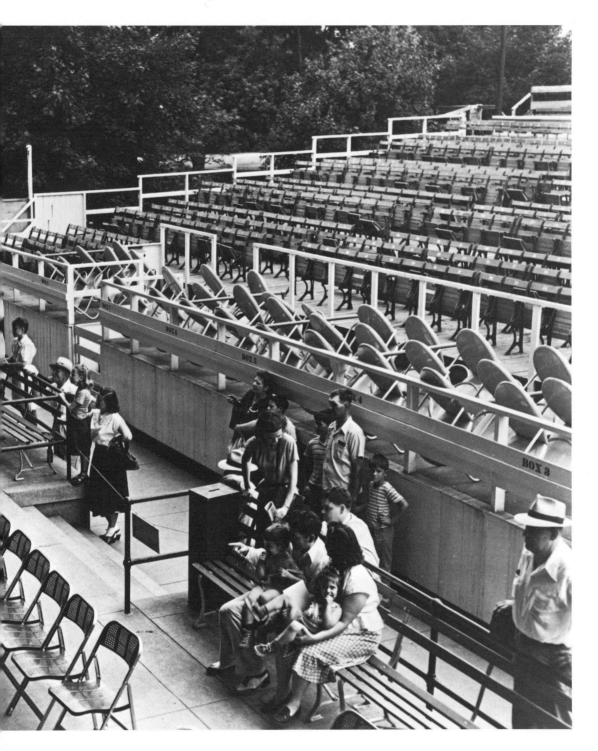

at City Opera, but the company's management continued to regard her more as a workhorse than a star. That attitude made itself emphatically clear when City Opera planned its first official season at its new Lincoln Center headquarters. Opening in September 1966, the season would begin with Handel's *Julius Caesar*. Like her colleagues, Sills expected Julius Rudel to assign the role of Cleopatra to a City Opera soprano. She herself seemed the perfect candidate: Her appearances had attracted large audiences to City Opera, and her light, agile voice was uniquely suited to the part of Cleopatra.

Then, to her astonishment, she learned that Rudel had offered the Cleopatra role to Phyllis Curtin, a Metropolitan Opera soprano whose career had been launched at City Opera. Sills was stunned. She found it incredible that Rudel would go outside of the City Opera roster to find a leading singer for the grand opening of the company's new theater.

Confronting Rudel, she announced that unless she could sing Cleopatra, she would quit. At that point, with a hefty number of Sills performances on its fall schedule, City Opera needed her. Beverly Sills got the role.

Sills spent the summer of 1966 working on *Julius Caesar*. She rehearsed with bass Norman Treigle, who was to play Caesar, and with Julius Rudel, who would conduct the opera. She also spent many hours working with director Tito Capobianco and his wife, Gigi, a choreographer specializing in stage

Opera director Tito Capobianco (shown) helped Sills create an alluring Cleopatra for City Opera's production of Julius Caesar. *Her performance in the role brought her fame.*

movement. Under the guidance of the Capobiancos, Sills learned to make her Cleopatra the most feminine and seductive of creatures. Gigi Capobianco told her that she should never make a fast gesture, that she should think of herself as having feathers in her hands. In effect, she choreographed all Sills's movements, helping her to create a Cleopatra of alluring sensuality.

Opening night at City Opera finally arrived. There was no need for a yellow marker after Sills's performance in *Julius Caesar*. "What a night that was!" she told an interviewer in 1988. "At the end of the second act, while I was singing [the aria] *Se pieta*, I just knew that I had done something extraordinary vocally. That it was recognized was fabulous, but it really wouldn't have mattered. There was a feeling of elation I had after that performance that was enough in itself. We had brought the house down in other productions, but it wasn't the same. That night it was thunder, and more thunder. It was such an evening!"

Cleopatra was the breakthrough Sills had been dreaming of. Her performance of the role showed critics and audiences that she had a rare vocal gift. That night, she became the unquestioned prima donna of the New York City Opera. She also proved that her performances deserved international attention and acclaim. She was to get both—along with some problems she had not anticipated.

As Suor Angelica in a 1967 production of Puccini's Il Trittico, *Sills performed a role so close to her heart that she wept onstage.*

S I X

"The Greatest Singing Actress of Them All"

Applause ringing in her ears, Sills swept into her dressing room after her final curtain call as Cleopatra. Her husband and mother awaited her. "I want to hear somebody do what I just did," said the exultant star. "You never will," Shirley Silverman responded. "I took that for what it was worth," Sills wrote later, "which was plenty."

When the magical evening ended, Sills once again faced the reality of problems at home. Bucky, still unable to speak, was also subject to seizures and radical behavior changes, from totally inert to wildly hyperactive. Incapable of relating to other people, he had no playmates or activities, and he needed constant watching to keep him from hurting himself. Finally, his parents came to a wrenching decision: Bucky would have a better life in an institution.

In 1967, when Bucky was six years old, his parents brought him to a special school in Massachusetts. Although Sills knew the move was in her son's best interests, it almost broke her heart. "Peter and I," she recalled, "both knew that our son was leaving home forever." Writing about him 20 years later, she said, "Bucky is twenty-six now, and to me he's still a lovable little boy. Peter and I visit him once a month, and sometimes ... he puts his arm around me. That always makes me think there's something inside Bucky trying to come out." Two days after Bucky went to his new school, Sills starred in *Il Trittico*, a trio of one-act operas by the Italian composer Giacomo Puccini (1858–1924), at the New York City Opera. One of the three works, *Suor Angelica*, tells the story of an aristocratic woman who gives birth to an illegitimate baby. Forced to give up her child, she enters a convent, then learns that her baby has died. Sills had hoped that the hard work of rehearsing and presenting the three operas would ease her sorrow over parting with Bucky. Instead, she identified so closely with the character of Suor Angelica that she burst into tears during the performance. She vowed never to sing that role again. She never did.

Increasingly, Beverly Sills found that her career was both an escape from the problems at home and an outlet for the pain created by those problems. About this time, music critic Hubert Saal wrote a profile of Sills for the *New York Times Magazine.* Commenting on the change in her performances since her reappearance on the stage, he observed: "She returned a different artist. She made entrances in an aura of serene confidence. When she sang, melody just poured out without visible breath or facial distortion." Saal quoted Sills on her onstage transformation: "My own feelings are that after going through terribly trying times, I was released from a lot of fears. I felt that if I could survive this, I could survive anything."

The following fall, Julius Rudel called Sills into his office. He told her that during the coming year, City Opera would mount a new production of any opera in which she wanted to perform. The soprano, who had always loved French opera, immediately chose *Manon.* The delicacy of her voice, the grace of her singing style, and the fluency of her French made her particu-

larly well suited for the French repertoire. Sills immersed herself in the role of Manon. "I lived that girl for six months," she told an interviewer. "I ate her and breathed her; I really was obsessed with her."

Manon is a young countrywoman who is being sent to a convent by her family. At an inn on the way, she meets Des Grieux, a young, innocent aristocrat. Enchanted by Manon's beauty, Des Grieux persuades her to run off to Paris with him. In the second act, which finds the lovers in their modest Paris apartment, Des Grieux is writing to tell his father that he wants to marry Manon. The father, who hopes to talk his son out of his relationship with the lower-class Manon, has meanwhile arranged to have him kidnapped and brought home.

Manon's cousin arrives at the apartment to ask Des Grieux about his intentions toward Manon. With him is Bretigny, a rich man who tells Manon about the plans of Des Grieux's father and who offers her a glamorous life if she will come and live with him. Attracted by the thought of luxury, she does not protest. Des Grieux goes out to mail his letter, and Manon, alone for a few minutes, soliloquizes about the many beautiful moments she has shared with him despite their meager way of life. When Des Grieux returns, he is abducted.

As the third act opens on a crowded Paris boulevard, bystanders are dazzled by the sight of the exquisitely dressed Manon. Overhearing a conversation, she learns that Des Grieux, crushed by

As the title character in a City Opera presentation of Manon, *Sills played an innocent young woman corrupted by wealth. The opera was one of her favorites.*

Georges Massenet, great-grandnephew of Manon's *composer, Jules Massenet, joins Shirley Silverman and her daughter, Beverly Sills, after the singer's 1968 rendition of the opera.*

her desertion, is entering the priesthood. She rushes off to his seminary, where she succeeds in seducing him. In the last act, Manon is arrested on charges of prostitution. Weary and ill from her imprisonment, she asks Des Grieux's forgiveness for her pleasure-seeking ways and infidelity before she dies.

Sills brought a unique freshness and depth to Manon, a character who has been portrayed as everything from a vulnerable little creature to a cheap hussy. She thoroughly researched her part in order to create a full portrait of Manon. The year after the *Manon* premiere, Sills talked to an interviewer about her interpretation of the role: "The things she says, like 'My family

accuses me of having too much fun. What kind of fun could a girl like this have? First of all, she can't possibly come from a high-ranking family. She can't have come from a good family because the Momma put her on a coach and sent her unchaperoned all by herself—this little girl who liked fun too much—to put her in a convent because the family couldn't handle her. Also I suspect that because it was good to get one less mouth to feed. The girl probably dressed up once a week for church . . . put on shoes . . . other than that, she must have worked in the fields." The soprano probed Manon's character: "I don't think Manon's immoral. The question has been put to me whether I'm playing her as a pure girl when she comes on the stage. I am. Perhaps I'm wrong. If the mother is sending her off to a convent, there's still an attachment to the church, and obviously she hasn't gotten into serious trouble, but enough to get the mother nervous. I play her as a very inexperienced girl when she comes on."

As Manon, Sills provided moments that stayed with audiences long after the curtain fell: her first-act entrance as a wide-eyed, awkward young woman; her breathless repetition of *"à Paris"* (to Paris) when Des Grieux suggests that they run away together; her hushed second-act soliloquy about the dreams she shared with her lover; her brilliant singing as the glamorous courtesan in the third act; her sensuous entwinement of Des Grieux in her flowing chiffon scarf during the seduction scene. Every night, she noted in her autobiography, "the public would go wild" when Des Grieux seized her scarf and buried his face in its perfumed folds.

Critics raved about Sills's Manon. "She was everything—handsome, a fine actress, a sex symbol, petulant, merry, naïve, and terribly, terribly knowing," said the New York Times. Newsweek magazine, which headlined its Sills story OPERA'S NEW SUPERSTAR, described her voice as one that "combines highness and strength, purity and color." The magazine's music critic went on to marvel at Sills's ability to sing "with her back to the audience as she mounts a steep staircase, or flat on her back in bed, or slumped on the floor hugging a table leg." What Julius Caesar had done to spotlight Sills's abilities as a singer and musician, Manon did to showcase her talent as a singing actress.

When Sills was growing up, many sopranos, including her idol, Lily Pons, sounded like virtuoso songbirds. They produced beautiful sounds, but they lacked a profound commitment to dramatic values. Maria Callas, (1923–77), a young Greek-American coloratura whose career blossomed in Europe in the 1950s, changed that approach almost single-handedly. Callas brought a deep emotional truth to her characterizations; her intensity and communicative powers gave opera new life.

Although Sills did not try to imitate Callas, she admired her, and she, too, knew how to act with her voice. Cou-

pled with her sense of drama was a sense of joy that made her performances unique. There was no evidence of effort or nerves when she was onstage. The immersion in character—which emanated not only from the thought that went into her roles but also from the sense of escape that she experienced onstage—was total.

Within a short time after the Manon opening on March 21, 1968, Beverly Sills became one of the most highly

Metropolitan Opera Company director Rudolf Bing (right) greets coloratura Maria Callas and her husband, Giovanni Meneghini, in 1958. Like Sills, Callas emphasized opera's dramatic qualities.

paid, most sought-after sopranos in the business. But fame, she discovered, could create problems. "You are under scrutiny the minute stardom hits you," she told an interviewer in 1988. "So is your family, and it can be a little bit painful. My daughter and I could never go shopping the way other mothers and daughters do. Even in the opera house itself, the relationship between colleagues changes. There was a kind of nudging, a 'let's see what she can do' attitude, always a competitive rather than an ensemble spirit among colleagues. And that took the fun out of it. That's why I always loved to come back to City Opera, to an ensemble company."

Sills soon found herself deluged with invitations to sing in opera houses around the globe. Until now, she had tended to accept every offer she received from major opera companies. Realizing that she needed guidance and advice in shaping her career, she hired Edgar Vincent, a respected public-relations consultant in the classical music industry, to be her manager. From then on, Vincent was to supervise every aspect of Sills's professional life.

Early in 1969, Vincent received a phone call from Thomas Schippers, an American conductor who was preparing a new production of *The Siege of Corinth* by the Italian composer Gioac-

Sills sings an aria during a shipboard scene in The Siege of Corinth, *the opera in which she made her debut at Italy's famed La Scala.*

chino Rossini (1792–1868). The opera was scheduled for presentation in April at La Scala, the celebrated opera house in Milan, Italy. Schippers told Vincent that the soprano originally signed for Pamira, the lead role in Rossini's opera, was pregnant and unable to perform. What he desperately needed, the conductor said, was a tremendously gifted, Italian-speaking, quick-learning soprano who could to fly to Italy at once. Without hesitation, Vincent recommended Beverly Sills.

La Scala was—and is—considered the most important opera house in the world; to debut there is to arrive at the pinnacle of opera. For the past two centuries, the world's finest singers have performed at La Scala, and Italy's greatest composers have written operas specifically for its stage. Furthermore, Pamira was an excellent part, well suited to Sills's voice. When Schippers asked her take the role, she said yes. "If you sing well at La Scala, God smiles on your career," she observed. "Every opera singer knows this."

When the soprano arrived for rehearsals at the splendid scarlet-and-ivory theater, she sensed a touch of hostility from the La Scala crew. At first unsure what was expected of her, Sills quickly learned after a series of encounters with the costume department. One of her costumes had been made of gold lamé to suit the previous soprano. Sills found it unsuitable for her coloring; she preferred silver, and the costume designer agreed. Yet at every rehearsal the wardrobe mistress arrived with the same gold costume. Sills gently reminded

her that she had requested silver; the seamstress told her not to worry. Next rehearsal: the gold costume.

Finally, Sills helped herself to the wardrobe mistress's scissors. As the chorus watched in silence, she cut the gold costume in half. The singers applauded and cheered. Next rehearsal: a silver costume. Obviously, the La Scala regulars had been waiting for Sills to assert herself, to prove she was worthy of the honor of singing at Milan's famous opera house. Such displays were not Sills's style, but if La Scala wanted a temperamental prima donna, the cheerful, outgoing redhead from Brooklyn could play the part as well as anyone.

Before the premiere, Sills knew she had earned the respect of La Scala's regulars—as an artist and as a temperamental prima donna. At one rehearsal, the orchestra in the pit gave her a standing ovation after her major aria. Applause from the orchestra is a rarity in any opera house; an ovation of this kind had not occurred at La Scala in more than 50 years. And on opening night, the chief of the women in the chorus came to Sills's dressing room with a gift from all of them. She told the American singer that the cast was praying for her success—another extremely unusual gesture from the professionals at La Scala.

The performance was an enormous success. In tribute to Sills's La Scala debut, *Newsweek* put her on the cover of its April 21, 1969, issue, entitling the story "La Sills at the Summit." The magazine described her performance as

La Scala (above), built in Milan, Italy, in 1788, has traditionally been considered the world's premier opera house. Opera originated in Italy in the 17th century.

"flawless" and the audience response as "tumultuous." It said Sills's singing of Pamira's major aria was "a Fourth of July fireworks, her voice heated to the point of incandescence, tossing off run after run with perfect intonation." *Newsweek*, which proclaimed Sills "the greatest prima donna of our time" and "the greatest singing actress of them all," also mentioned her "great personal tragedy, which, instead of disabling her has propelled her to the pinnacle of her art."

At this point, Sills was as well known to the general public as she was to opera lovers. Learning her personal history, Americans came to admire her courage, optimism, and ready laughter. Her image was that of prima donna with a difference. She was a star, but she was open and spontaneous, and her roles as wife and mother endowed her with a sense of proportion and equilibrium that people found appealing. Everyone—from stagehands to total strangers who waited for her at the stage door—called her Beverly.

To Americans, Beverly Sills had become something of a national treasure. Ironically, America's preeminent opera house, the Met, had yet to invite her to its hallowed stage.

Sills performs the mad scene in Donizetti's Lucia di Lammermoor.
After her 1969 success as Lucia, the soprano recalled, she "went mad all over the world."

SEVEN

Lincoln Center Star

I'm the wallflower who's become the belle of the ball," said Beverly Sills to an interviewer in the summer of 1969. Was she surprised by her sudden leap into stardom? "No," said the 40-year-old soprano. "I worked very hard and when my time came I was prepared for it. I feel I'm getting what is my due."

In 1969, Peter Greenough retired from his newspaper job. Because life would be much easier for Sills if she lived close to City Opera, the couple decided to move to Manhattan. With their daughter Muffy, they settled into a spacious apartment on the Upper West Side. Sills was happy to quit commuting; she was back where she belonged.

Bucky still lived at a special school in Massachusetts, Lindley was at Bennington College in Vermont, and Nancy, who had enrolled at Barnard College in Manhattan, had taken her own apartment. Muffy, meanwhile, was making excellent progress. She had learned to speak and to function in a hearing society. Much to her mother's delight, the 10-year-old girl enjoyed going to the opera; although she could not hear the music, she loved the spectacle and the onstage action.

That fall, Sills enjoyed another overwhelming success at City Opera. This time she sang the title role in *Lucia di Lammermoor*, by Italian composer Gaetano Donizetti (1797–1848). Based on Sir Walter Scott's novel *The Bride of Lammermoor*, Donizetti's opera tells the tragic story of a young Scotswoman. Forced to abandon her lover and marry a man she does not love, she goes insane and murders her new husband. *Lucia* is celebrated for its dramatic "mad scene," in which the heroine carries a bloodstained knife and sings a long scene full of scales, trills, and vocal leaps that portray her unhinged mind.

Italian composers Gioacchino Rossini, Vincenzo Bellini, and Gaetano Donizetti (clockwise from top left) are best known for their bel canto operas, which showcase lyrical singing.

Lucia di Lammermoor is part of the operatic repertoire known as *bel canto*, "beautiful singing" in Italian. Bel canto operas are the work of early 19th-century Italian composers, primarily Gioacchino Rossini, Vincenzo Bellini (1801–35), and Gaetano Donizetti. The singers who interpret these operas must be able to produce a pure, lovely sound while singing music ranging from very high to low in the voice with ease and flexibility. Requiring the same vocal agility as Handel's works, bel canto also calls for an Italianate warmth, richness of sound, and directness of expression.

Sills fell in love with Lucia, immersing herself in the character so completely that when the curtain fell after the opening performance, she was in tears. And the critics, in turn, loved Sills's Lucia. Her performance, especially in the mad scene, drew not only rave reviews but a flood of invitations to repeat the role in other opera houses worldwide. "For the next few years," noted Sills later, "I found myself going mad all over the world." She sang Lucia in London, Boston, Mexico City, Shreveport, San Francisco, Buenos Aires, and Milan. The following February, Sills sang the title role in a Donizetti comic opera, *The Daughter of the Regiment*. A natural for comedy, Sills was perfectly cast as Marie, a young tomboy who has been raised by the soldiers of an army regiment. Her timing was superb, and she made Marie's music sound like her own infectious laughter. When she sang the role with the Opera Company of Bos-

ton, however, her first performance turned out to be funnier than anyone expected.

The unplanned hilarity came from a scene in which Marie's aunt, who is trying to make a "lady" of her, gives her a singing lesson as the sergeant of the regiment looks on. In the Boston production, a metronome marked the tempo of Marie's song, giving out the sound of a cuckoo every eight beats. When the song was over, Sills was supposed to shut off the metronome and continue with the scene. It worked during rehearsal. But when Sills turned off the metronome during the first performance, it not only refused to stop, it cuckooed on each beat.

Every time she tried to resume singing, the metronome cuckooed again. The audience was hysterical with laughter, and Sills was close to joining them. Then the baritone who played the sergeant gallantly walked over and fixed the metronome. The audience applauded and the opera continued— almost. As soon as the cast began to sing, the metronome sounded its cuckoo call. By this time, Sills was laughing as hard as the audience. But the baritone was undaunted. He threw the unruly metronome on the floor and stomped on it. The audience cheered; he stepped away from the metronome, and one last time, it cuckooed.

Finally, Sills picked it up and handed it to a member of the orchestra who hurled it under the stage. In later years, Sills would sing *The Daughter of the Regiment* many times, but obviously, she always considered the Boston per-

Sills belts out an aria in The Daughter of the Regiment. *A gifted comedian, the soprano thoroughly enjoyed the part of Marie in Donizetti's comic opera.*

Britain's Queen Elizabeth I (pictured), subject of Donizetti's opera Roberto Devereux, *enjoyed wearing ornate hair ornaments and elaborately jeweled gowns.*

Attired as Elizabeth, Sills displays an uncanny resemblance to the historical queen. The soprano called the role her "greatest artistic challenge."

formance of this role her most memorable.

Roberto Devereux, the next Donizetti opera Sills learned, was on a totally different plane. This work focuses on the love affair between Elizabeth I, the queen who ruled England from 1558 to 1603, and the much younger earl of Essex, Robert Devereux. When Elizabeth discovers that Essex loves someone else, the bitter, heartbroken Queen orders his execution.

Determined to create an accurate, emotionally honest portrayal of the proud monarch, Sills devoured a huge stack of books about Elizabeth and her era. The soprano's jewel-encrusted costumes were based on portraits of the historical queen. One of the outfits, at 55 pounds, proved heavy enough to stand up by itself on the dressing-room floor, and too heavy to be lifted over the singer's head. To don the garment, Sills had to step into it and then wait for two dressers to hoist it into place. Performing in that costume was "no picnic," she noted. Her makeup, so complex that it took two and a half hours to apply, included chalk-white face paint accented with black lines.

Under the stage lights, it turned Sills into a harsh old woman.

The more Sills rehearsed the role, the more eager she was to perform it. But her joyous anticipation of opening night was marred by a sad event: the death of Estelle Liebling. "The news left me numb," said Sills. Liebling, who had served as Sills's teacher and mentor for 34 years, was 91 years old, but until her final illness a few months earlier, she had continued to be the soprano's frankest critic. In later years, Sills wrote that "there were times when I'd sing especially well and I'd think: *Teacher would have liked that.*"

Roberto Devereux, which had not been staged in America since 1851, opened at City Opera on October 15, 1970. Playing opposite Sills was tenor Placido Domingo, then almost unknown but soon to become one of the most popular opera stars in the world. Domingo, said Sills, was not only a fine musician, but a "real trouper." In the second act, the furious queen pushes Essex to his knees and slaps his face resoundingly. Immersed in her role, Sills sometimes forgot to soften the blow; at such moments, reported Sills, "Placi didn't blink an eye."

Sills had hoped for a success; she got a triumph. At the end of act 2, the audience gave her a tumultuous standing ovation, the first she had ever received in the middle of an opera and a remarkable tribute for any singer. Sills said Elizabeth was the most difficult role she ever sang. But she loved the part, which she considered the greatest artistic achievement of her career. It was as Elizabeth that Sills, identified as "America's Queen of Opera," appeared on the cover of *Time* magazine in late 1971. Entitled "Beverly Sills: the Fastest Voice Alive," the *Time* story reported the soprano's extensive preparation for playing Elizabeth, marveled at her impressively high IQ, and praised the depth and "bite" of her acting.

During the early 1970s, Sills recorded *Roberto Devereux* and many of her other successful roles. The albums were best-sellers on the classical music market, but Sills found them frustrating: The elements that made her live performances compelling simply could not be captured on recordings. Discussing *Roberto Devereux* with an interviewer, she said, "There were pauses on stage that meant more than 65 pages of music. For instance, after Elizabeth slaps Essex, I would slowly and silently walk up to the throne with my back to the audience. Elizabeth aged during the 10 seconds it took to do that. On records, my voice sounds exactly the same when she begins to sing again after the slap. But on stage, after I had made that long walk and turned around, the audience was not listening to my voice any more. They were watching an aged woman. That's the kind of effect I could never get on records."

Two months after *Roberto Devereux*, Sills, accompanied by her husband and daughter, flew to England for her debut with London's Royal Opera at Covent Garden. British audiences greeted her *Lucia* warmly, but the British press was less than friendly. After a

London's elegant Covent Garden (above), home of the Royal Opera, failed to impress Sills; she found its costumes threadbare, its staff chilly, and its reviewers hostile.

group of American tourists sent flowers to the stage at the close of Sills's famed "mad scene," London observers snidely referred to the singer as "Miss America Superstar." One critic even said, "I wonder how much her husband had to pay to let her sing here?" Sills probably understated the case when she said she "wound up with very little respect for English opera critics."

The visiting American was also displeased by coolness of Covent Garden's staff and by the dilapidated sets and costumes furnished for *Lucia*. She remained fond of London and its people, but she made up her mind never again to sing in its opera house. "Professionally speaking," she noted in her autobiography, "Covent Garden was a nice place to visit, but I was glad I didn't live there."

Between performances of *Lucia*, Sills went to West Germany, where she sang a *Traviata* at Berlin's Deutsche Oper, then on to Paris for a concert. Her reception in Paris was quite different from that in London. "If I do say so myself," Sills reminisced happily, "I tore Paris apart—audience, reviews, everything was *formidable*." But she admitted that her fluency in French helped. "The French they are a funny race," she said, "but they do prefer people who can speak their language well."

Impresarios (opera producers) in Germany and England offered Sills contracts to return to Europe, but she declined. Her professional home was the New York City Opera, which had thrived since its move to Lincoln Center. City Opera was no longer a poor cousin to the Met, tucked away in the old City Center theater. The company had become a vibrant, viable organization featuring world-class singers and well-directed productions. Loyalty to City Opera was not the only factor, however, that shaped Sills's decisions about her career. "Even when the opportunity presented itself for a great international career, I could never take advantage of it," she told an interviewer in 1988.

Looking back at the evolution of her professional life, she said, "I really didn't feel I could afford to dream of an international career because of my five children and a husband who required a great deal of tender loving care and attention. He wanted a wife. All the European decisions were based on the children's school schedules. That was a decision I had to make, but it wasn't for lack of offers. I broke the European myth: I could have a great career without Europe. I broke another myth; that is that I had a fabulous reception in Europe in the great opera houses there without ever stepping on the stage of the Met."

That situation would soon change. In the meantime, Sills was off to Washington, D.C.: In February 1971, President Richard Nixon invited her to perform at the White House. Although she did not share Nixon's political views, she accepted out of respect for the office of the president.

The recital for the first family and their guests took place in the elegant East Room of the White House. Sills's

Flanked by President Richard Nixon and his wife, Pat, Sills wears a long velvet coat. Without it, she said, her 1971 White House performance might have become "a striptease."

family—her husband, daughter, mother, and her brothers and their wives— watched with pride as she made her entrance in a shimmering white gown, but they were puzzled by what she did after her third piece: She backed off the stage, then returned wearing her long red-velvet evening coat. The room was not chilly, and observers thought Sills's action peculiar, to say the least.

When the soprano neared the end of her performance, she decided to tell the audience what the coat was all about. Shortly after her entrance, the zipper on her dress popped, opening her gown all the way down the back. "I grabbed the front of the gown just as gravity was about to turn my recital into a striptease," she joked later. Luckily, she had the coat to cover herself up for the rest of the evening. Sills became a White House favorite under each succeeding administration, both as a performer and a guest at gala dinners there.

Soon after Sills's first evening at the White House, she received a request from the March of Dimes: Would she become national chair of its fundraising operation, the Mothers' March on Birth Defects? Sills had long ad-

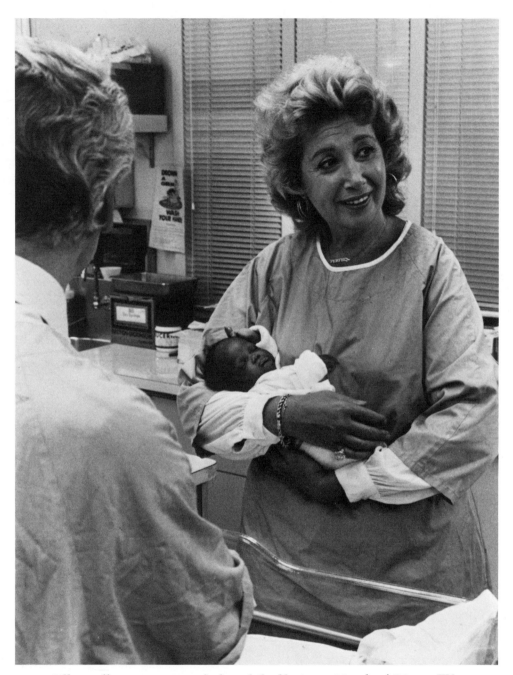

Sills cradles a premature baby while filming a March of Dimes TV appeal. The singer helped raise thousands of dollars to combat birth defects.

mired the March of Dimes for its successful battle against poliomyelitis (a paralyzing disease commonly known as polio); birth defects were, of course, of great interest to her. After discussing the position with Muffy, Sills agreed to take it.

Sills found the work—traveling around the country, giving speeches and interviews, and meeting with handicapped children and their parents—both agonizing and deeply rewarding. Her direct approach and her willingness to share her deeper feelings with other parents made her immediately accessible to the people she spoke to and made her efforts immensely successful.

Sills's professional life took on a busy but manageable rhythm. She recorded overseas during the summers, sang with City Opera each fall and spring, and scheduled appearances in other cities in between. Then, during a City Opera performance in the fall of 1974, she was holding a high note when she was suddenly hit by excruciating abdominal pain. She cut off the note, and the audience gasped. She sat down, the pain passed, and she finished her performance.

The next morning, Sills telephoned her brother, Dr. Sidney Silverman. On his recommendation, she went to see a gynecologist. After a series of tests, she left for Dallas, where she was scheduled to sing Donizetti's *Lucrezia Borgia*. Two days later, her brother called to tell her she had cancer.

Peter Greenough flew to Dallas and brought his wife back to New York City, where she was operated on for an ovarian tumor. The surgeon removed it completely; Sills's prospects for survival, he said, were excellent, and she would need no further treatment. Now it was just a matter of patience during the recuperative process. Sills was very weak, and her visitors noticed how frail she had become. Aware that many people think of cancer as a death sentence, she was afraid her colleagues would think she was dying. "I just was not going to let that happen," she recalled.

Contrary to her doctor's orders, she began walking. She did breathing exercises and vocalized very gently each day. Then she told her doctor that she planned to leave the hospital in two weeks to begin rehearsing for a San Francisco production of *The Daughter of the Regiment*. The doctor laughed. "That's not even worth discussing," he said. "That's what *he* thought," noted the determined Sills.

In agonizing pain, she managed to get through the rehearsals and the performances. In *Beverly*, she mused about why she had put herself through such an ordeal. "The plain truth is," she concluded, "that if I had canceled, *I* would have worried that I was dying. . . . I'm still glad I did what I did. I sang all my performances. I beat the pain."

The following spring, Sills made new headlines: At long last, she debuted at the Metropolitan Opera. It was then 20 years since she had first appeared with the New York City Opera, 6 years after her La Scala debut, and 5 years since she sang at London's Covent Garden.

Why had her Met debut taken so long? The answer, Sills explained in *Bubbles*, consisted of "three words: Sir Rudolf Bing."

General manager of the Met from 1950 until 1972, the Austrian-born Bing "had a thing about American singers," said Sills. The more the press and the Met's board of trustees quizzed Bing about his reasons for excluding Sills, the more entrenched his attitude became. Although Sills received incessant requests from reporters to talk, as she put it, about "'poor little Bubbles' from Brooklyn being blackballed" from the Met, she refused to discuss the issue. But, she noted in her autobiography, Bing's hostility proved to be an asset. "In an odd way, Mr. Bing made my career by keeping me out of the Met so long," she said. "Nothing infuriates the American public quite as much as the notion of a haughty, foreign-born aristocrat being mean to one of its native-born girls."

After Bing finally resigned, his successor invited Sills to debut at the Met. She agreed. The date was set for April 7, 1975; Sills would sing Pamira in *The Siege of Corinth*, the opera that had brought her such acclaim in Milan. Ticket requests for Sills's debut, a benefit for the Met, flooded the box office.

Tenor Justino Diaz embraces Sills during her Metropolitan Opera debut in The Siege of Corinth. *Her appearance on the Met stage was greeted with thunderous applause.*

Ranging in price from $60 to $500, the tickets quickly sold out, disappointing thousands of opera fans.

Sills and her costars, mezzo-soprano Shirley Verrett and tenor Justino Diaz, were somewhat nervous about the public's high expectations for the performance. In *Bubbles*, Sills recalled one rehearsal when she said she hoped the three of them could live up to all the publicity. "How can we miss?" joked Diaz. "I'm a Puerto Rican, Shirley is black, and you're a Jew. We've cornered the market on minorities. Who would *dare* criticize us?"

On the day of the debut an avalanche of flowers arrived. Although Sills claims that her friends were more excited by the occasion than she was, she would never forget stepping onto the stage on opening night. The moment the audience caught sight of her, it burst into an earsplitting roar. Among the clapping, cheering fans were Sills's husband, daughter, mother, and her brothers and their wives; opera stars Robert Merrill and Risë Stevens; and Hollywood stars Kirk Douglas and Danny Kaye. When the final curtain fell, the excited crowd gave Sills an 18-minute standing ovation. Both she and the audience, she said later, seemed to feel "that a longstanding wrong had been righted."

Called "a superoccasion" by the Associated Press, Sills's Met debut was reported across the nation. "During nearly 20 minutes of curtain calls at the end," said the wire service story, "fans showered the coloratura with bits of metal foil, confetti and rose petals." The *New York Times* raved about Sills's "beauty of tone and infinite feeling." *Newsweek*'s report summed up the event: "What the fuss was really about was not her debut with the Met but the Met's debut with Beverly Sills."

Beverly Sills was now the star of two major opera houses. Although many City Opera performers have become major singers at the Met, very few have continued to sing at both. Recognition of Sills's achievements came from far beyond the opera world. Newly elected president Jimmy Carter invited her to sing at his inauguration gala; Temple University, New York University, the New England Conservatory of Music, and Harvard awarded her honorary degrees.

Sills's natural effervescence and quick wit made her a television favorite. She was equally at ease chatting with Merv Griffin, singing a ballad on Johnny Carson's "The Tonight Show," performing a song-and-dance routine with Carol Burnett, or bantering with the Muppets. The soprano's down-to-earth style helped to humanize opera singers and make opera more accessible to the general public: Fans often came backstage after her opera performances to say that her television appearances had inspired them to come and see her perform. On such occasions, she felt she had chalked up more victories for the art of opera.

Both the Metropolitan Opera and City Opera mounted new productions for Sills, and other major companies continued to offer her contracts. Then, in 1977, an unexpected offer came from City Opera: The company, which had been experiencing administrative difficulties, asked her to join Julius Rudel as codirector. Sills knew that her friend Rudel had long wanted more free time to guest-conduct with other orchestras; after discussing the proposal with him, she agreed to take the job in the fall of 1980. Then Rudel decided to retire early, in June 1979.

The chairman of the City Opera board asked Sills to take over. She said yes. At the height of her success, she had already decided to stop singing.

Arm in arm with her predecessor, Julius Rudel, Beverly Sills beams as she takes over her new role: general director of the New York City Opera.

E I G H T

On the Brink of Disaster

Beverly Sills's decision to retire from singing was based on several factors. Most important, she wanted to spend more time with her family, particularly with Muffy. And she no longer possessed the physical and vocal stamina to sing the demanding roles, such as Elizabeth I, that she loved best. Her performances continued to be extraordinary, but the human voice is a fragile instrument, and hers, which had always been light, had begun to lose some of its former sheen and power.

Operatic production, as well as operatic singing, had always fascinated Sills. As early as 1974, she had talked to Julius Rudel about eventually becoming an administrator. Now, in June 1979, more than a year before the retirement date she had planned, she found herself general director of the New York City Opera. In order to carry out the responsibilities of her new position, she canceled as many of her concert and operatic appearances as possible.

During her first season as general director, in 1979, Beverly Sills gave her last performance at City Opera. *La Loca* (the lunatic, in Spanish) was written for Sills by the contemporary composer Gian Carlo Menotti. The opera, which tells the tragic story of a 16th-century Spanish queen, ends with a highly dramatic mad scene. Sills loved it. "Aside from my Queen Elizabeth in *Roberto Devereux*," she said in her autobiography, "*La Loca* was the best piece of acting I've ever done." The audience obviously agreed, applauding endlessly and showering the soprano with flowers at the final curtain. Acknowledging her devoted fans, Sills said only a few simple words: "I just want to thank you for a wonderful love affair, and the best is yet to come."

Sills's achievements were honored by the nation the following June, when

President Carter awarded her the Presidential Medal of Freedom. Carter presented the medal—the country's highest peacetime civilian award—on the vast South Lawn of the White House. "Beverly Sills," he said, "has captured with her voice every note of human feeling, and with her superb dramatic talent projected them out to us with ringing clarity.... She has touched and delighted audiences throughout the world as a performer, as a recording artist, and now as a producer—and of all her arts she is truly a master."

Gian Carlo Menotti (below) wrote La Loca *specifically for Sills. He also composed the popular Christmas opera* Amahl and the Night Visitors.

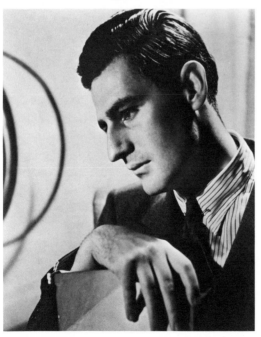

At a farewell gala that October, Sills made her last appearance as a prima donna. The event, a benefit for the New York City Opera, was held both to toast Sills and to raise money for the financially troubled company. With tickets selling for as much as $1,000 each, the theater was sold out; net receipts amounted to more than $1 million. The evening's performance consisted of one act of *Die Fledermaus*, the Viennese opera in which Sills made her New York debut, and featured a dazzling array of stars from the worlds of opera, Broadway, and Hollywood.

Tenor Placido Domingo, baritone Sherrill Milnes, and sopranos Renata Scotto and Leontyne Price, mainstays of the Met roster, sang; old-time Broadway stars Mary Martin and Ethel Merman belted out show tunes; popular classical flutist James Galway played "Danny Boy." As the orchestra broke into a waltz, Sills took turns dancing with television commentator Walter Cronkite, New York mayor Edward Koch, actor Burt Reynolds, and New York Philharmonic conductor Zubin Mehta. At the show's climax, comedian Carol Burnett raced onto the stage and shouted, "What the hell happened to Gay Vienna?" Then she and Sills teamed up for a duet that brought the house down.

Sills closed the program as she had always closed her recitals: She sang a simple Portuguese lullaby that Estelle Liebling had arranged for her many years earlier. Sills had written special lyrics for the occasion:

President Jimmy Carter presents Sills with the Presidential Medal of Freedom. Carter said of the performer, "Of all her arts she is truly a master."

We have shared so much together
Tis not the end but a new start
So, my dears, you know I love you
You'll be forever in my heart.

The audience screamed and applauded. As Sills took her curtain calls, hundreds of multicolor balloons cascaded onto the stage, ending the celebration of an extraordinary career.

As a prima donna, Sills had become accustomed to crowds of adoring fans and eager impresarios, to dressing rooms overflowing with flowers and well-wishers. And she had always made a point of dressing for her role, sweeping into the theater in elegant fur coats, silk dresses, diamonds, and carefully applied makeup.

As City Opera's general director, she looked as glamorous as ever, her hair still perfectly coiffed, her outfits stunning as always. But nothing else was the same. When she arrived at the stage door for her first day as chief executive, she headed in a new direction. Instead of pushing the elevator button for the stage level, she walked down a long ramp to the company's subterranean business quarters and entered the windowless office she would share with two assistants. Dark, decorated with dreary linoleum and exposed heating

Carol Burnett (left) and Beverly Sills team up for a rousing duet. The two entertainers brought the house down at Sills's 1979 farewell gala.

pipes, Sills's basement workplace seemed miles away from the glittering world of spotlights and stage sets above it.

Within a short time, time, however, Sills claimed the anteroom right next door—a room that preserved her star image. It was small and charming, decorated with antiques, plants, and paintings, as well as posters that documented her career. Dominating the room was a gift from the San Diego Opera Guild: a hand-sewn quilt, each square illustrating one of her famous roles. In this anteroom, Sills could meet and talk privately with members of the staff, performers, and reporters. Her meetings always began with the sound of her coffee grinder as she prepared fresh coffee for her guests before settling down to business.

Sills attacked the job of general director with her usual energy and optimism, but it proved more daunting than she expected. Even before she assumed her new position, her efforts met criticism. She had announced her plan to keep the company mostly American, giving native-born performers opportunities they could once find primarily in Europe. Along with a letter denouncing Sills's plan as "protectionist," the *New York Times* published a cartoon that showed an obviously Germanic singer attired in a Valkyrie costume and standing in line at the unemployment office.

Sills had always found it easy to get along with her colleagues, and she assumed it would be the same now. "One of my goals," she recalled in *Beverly*, "was to show the world that you don't have to be a bastard to run an opera company. I was going to accomplish everything with a great big grin. I actually did that for about nine months." The turning point came in the spring of 1980, when the company mounted a new production of Mozart's *Don Giovanni*: "That's when I realized I had to wise up," she said, "and stop being nice, cheerful Beverly."

Decisions about opera productions and casts are made years in advance; Sills's input on artistic matters would not be evident before 1981. Nevertheless, she was now in charge and would be blamed for any problems that arose. In *Don Giovanni*, which had already been planned and designed by the time Sills took over City Opera, the statue of a murdered man appears on stage. The opera's director had decided to use a microphone to amplify the voice of the man who sang the statue's role. When Sills realized the singer was miked, she objected. She knew the sound equipment in the opera house was not sophisticated enough for such a purpose, and she was sure the singer's voice would carry without amplification. She ordered the microphone removed. Without her knowledge, the stage manager left it in place.

At the performance, Sills was shocked to hear the microphone used during the opera's crucial graveyard scene; as she had predicted, the theater's ancient amplification system creaked and groaned, then produced an explosive boom, creating a commotion in the theater. The scene was ruined.

Sills enjoys a quiet moment in her office at the New York State Theater. As the head of City Opera, Sills was determined to save the company from financial ruin.

When the curtain fell, a furious Sills raced backstage and berated the stage manager for disregarding her orders. The crew looked shocked, but Sills had learned an essential lesson: The general director of an opera company has to be tough.

Because Sills lacked administrative experience, her skills as a business executive were challenged continually. When she took over the company, she recalled in *Beverly*, "What I got was a lot of criticism that, at its heart, was antifemale: here was a woman doing a man's job, and she obviously was going to fall on her face. The put-downs had a snide tone to them that was hard to miss. . . . I felt like the woman in that song by Sting: Every breath I took, every move I made—people were watching me. And clucking their disapproval."

Not all Sills's early productions came up to her—or the public's—high expectations. Composer Kurt Weill's *Silverlake* worked out well; so did Sigmund Romberg's *Student Prince* and Bizet's *Pearl Fishers*. However, Sills later noted, Italo Montemezzi's *Love of Three Kings* "got roasted," and the company "really got crucified" for Jacques Offenbach's *Grand Duchess of Gerolstein*. But "for sheer catastrophe," she added, "you couldn't top our production of Verdi's *I Lombardi*." In this case, the lead soprano developed vocal fatigue, the backdrops designed for the production never arrived, and the revolving stage squeaked; each time it moved, the audience roared with laughter. During the curtain calls, the laughs became boos. And the next day, said Sills, "the critics slaughtered us."

There was an explanation for these disasters: City Opera's finances were in a state of chaos. Sills had unknowingly inherited a company that was $4 million in debt and on the edge of bankruptcy. "From the moment I became general director," she recalled later, "I found myself constantly in a life-or-death pursuit of money." Obviously, that pursuit allowed her little time to supervise the company's productions, which suffered as a result.

On the strength of Sills's personality and her reputation as a performer, she raised enough cash to keep the company afloat during her first year as general director. The 1981 spring season was praised for two new Sills productions: *Attila*, a rarely performed Verdi opera; and *The Cunning Little Vixen*, a neglected masterpiece by the Czechoslovakian composer Leoš Janáček (1854–1928). For *Vixen*, Sills asked Maurice Sendak, the prize-winning writer-illustrator of such popular children's books as *Where the Wild Things Are*, to design the sets and costumes. The charming, colorful production, noted Sills with satisfaction, was a *"big,* big hit."

The next season, however, was far from successful. Brochures announcing the upcoming operas went pouring out; ticket orders came trickling in. The drop in attendance resulted largely from two factors: Sills had decided to fight the growing financial crisis by raising ticket prices; regular City Opera patrons balked at the increase. Also, and probably even more important, City Opera's top drawing card for many years, Sills herself, was no longer singing.

Sills and her management of the company began to draw scathing press comments. In a 1982 article entitled "City Opera Searches for Stability," *New York Times* music critic John Rockwell wrote: "Both inside and outside the company, people are wondering about the City Opera's artistic purpose and financial stability. . . . In short, the honeymoon is over and Miss Sills must address herself to a number of serious problems." Rockwell went on to discuss the huge deficit, the drop in attendance, the decline in backstage morale, and the company's deteriorating performance standards. "Despite all this," he added wonderingly, "Miss Sills remains brightly optimistic."

Sills *had* to appear optimistic; she knew she could not raise funds for a company if she herself seemed defeated by its problems. But artistically, the season could not have been worse. The *New York Times* summed up the season's performances as "ragged and unpredictable." The *Village Voice*

Preparing for a 1980 City Opera production of Kurt Weill's 1933 opera, Silverlake, *Sills and musical-comedy star Joel Grey look over the script.*

claimed: "If things go on as they have been, the New York City Opera will lose all credibility with its artists, its audience, and its funding sources, and may have to fold."

The New York City Opera—the company that had nurtured Sills's singing career, the company that had made her a star, the company that "meant everything" to her—was in a state of financial and artistic collapse. And the only one who could do anything about it was Beverly Sills. She would have to take risky steps. Either they would work, or City Opera would close its doors permanently.

The costumes and sets for Sills's 1981 production of The Cunning Little Vixen *were designed by Maurice Sendak, author of many best-selling children's books.*

*A glittering opening-night audience packs the New York State Theater
for* Cendrillon, *the first of Sills's successful 1982 City Opera productions.*

NINE

A Golden Era Begins

Beverly Sills was not accustomed to failure. Working long and hard since childhood, she had achieved the imposing status of prima donna; faced with heartbreak as an adult, she had not only coped but triumphed. Now, at the age of 53, Sills was not about to give in to the formidable challenges—a string of recent artistic fiascos and a legacy of staggering debt—that faced her at City Opera.

Her advisers told her to accept the fact that the New York City Opera was drowning in debt. Even her financial-expert husband, Peter Greenough, believed the company should declare bankruptcy. Sills stubbornly refused, devising plans that would give her time to raise desperately needed money and to improve performance standards.

Her first move was to discard City Opera's tradition of running two separate seasons; the company would now offer a single stretch of productions from July through November. This plan eliminated the need for two expensive rehearsal periods and for the duplication of such start-up costs as advertising and subscription brochures. And a summer season, Sills reasoned, would attract the tourists who flocked to the city during the warm months. Because the Met was closed all summer, City Opera would have no competition. Sills's plan would also provide the additional time she needed, from the end of the fall 1982 season until July 1983, to organize the company's finances and to make production decisions.

The opera-going public responded to the new schedule enthusiastically: By the spring of 1983, City Opera had sold more than $1 million worth of season tickets. Hoping to please even more people, Sills experimented with another innovation: supertitles. This device, also called surtitles, consists of an above-stage screen on which transla-

And you, prepare her carriage.
You'll be her coachman.

Sills first brought supertitles to City Opera as an experiment. The innovation proved so popular that she made them a regular feature.

tions of the singers' words appear. Sills tried supertitles during a production of Jules Massenet's *Cendrillon* and polled the audience afterward. The reaction among operagoers was so positive that Sills installed supertitles permanently. Now in common use among opera companies, supertitles were radical at the time; generations of listeners had sat through countless hours of opera without understanding a word they heard. Confident that the new technology would increase attendance, Sills happily looked forward to the 1983 season, which would open on July 7.

Then, just before opening night, the orchestra went on strike. Because its members usually supplemented their incomes by playing at summer festivals, they objected to performing at

City Opera during the summer months. They also wanted the number of their weekly performances reduced from six to five. Sills promised to find other supplementary work for the musicians (which she eventually did), but the union leaders remained adamantly opposed to the single season and the six-performance week. Sills held her ground. Finally, after 54 days of bitter negotiations, the strike ended with a compromise: The musicians would play during the summer season, giving five and one-half performances each week.

City Opera's curtain finally rose on September 21. "Even though my first summer/fall season was shot to hell," Sills wrote later, "I was elated when the wrangling stopped and the music began again." The opera was *Cendrillon*, a retelling of the Cinderella story with a lustrous score by Jules Massenet, the French composer who also wrote *Manon*. A rarely heard gem, *Cendrillon* charmed audiences with its music and delighted them with its libretto: Thanks to the new supertitles, the meaning of every word was clear. Some critics found supertitles distracting, but audiences loved them. When the first New York City Opera audience was polled about its opinion of the titles, more than 90 percent of the respondents asked to have them continued.

The 1983 season proved successful; the 1984 season demonstrated, once and for all, that impresario Beverly Sills had mastered both the artistic and the administrative sides of her job. Con-

firming that view was a November 1984 *New York Times* story, written by music critic Donal Henahan:

> The New York City Opera, which began its 40th season 20 weeks ago in deep uncertainty, closes it this evening in the most confident frame of mind it has enjoyed in many years. . . . The mood is upbeat. This was the season in which Beverly Sills, the general director, decided to gamble on two extremely chancy innovations: the company's first summertime run and the first full season of subtitled or supertitled operas. Both gambles paid off heavily. Financially and administratively, the City Opera appears healthier than at any other time since Miss Sills took office. The general director, while never noted as a dispenser of gloom . . . positively exudes euphoria these days.

The New York City Opera had entered a new, golden era. By late summer 1985, Sills felt the company's future

A cluster of sparkling stars—Mary Martin (left), Carol Burnett (center), and Beverly Sills—attend an opera benefit party in the early 1980s.

was secure. She had pulled it from the brink of bankruptcy; she had enticed new audiences to the theater; she had revitalized the company with rarely heard operas, new productions, and a roster of winning young singers. She had even managed to get away from work on Labor Day weekend to spend some precious vacation time with her family at their summer home on Martha's Vineyard, an island summer resort off the coast of Massachusetts.

There, on Sunday, September 1, Sills received calamitous news: A flash fire in Passaic, New Jersey, had destroyed the warehouse in which the New York City Opera stored its costumes and props. More than 12,000 costumes were in ashes, as were the fans, hoops, jewelry, boots, swords, and other accessories necessary to every opera. Gone, too, were the costumes that meant most to Sills, the magnificent outfits she had worn as Queen Elizabeth and Cleopatra.

Sills listened to telephoned reports on the damage, then promised to fly back to New York and start to rebuild the opera company's inventory of costumes and props. Aware that an outburst from her would make her staff's spirits even lower, she tried to sound calm. But, she recalled, "after I said goodbye, I went into the bathroom and threw up."

Sills was devastated, but she refused to be defeated. "No one needed this fire, but it happened. It's done," she told an *Opera News* reporter. "But one thing is for sure. I won't be licked. I just don't take defeat. It's as simple as

that." The losses from the fire amounted to $10 million, but the costumes had been insured for only $1.5 million. A week after the fire, Sills established a Fire Emergency Fund; relentlessly stalking wealthy patrons and public-spirited corporations, she managed to raise $5 million— enough for the next season—by the end of the year. Vastly relieved, Sills said she now had only one worry: "That our sets will look 5,000 years old, while our costumes will look 5 *minutes* old."

During the next few seasons, life returned to normal, or as normal as life can be in an opera house. At most City Opera performances, Sills was a highly visible, redheaded presence, seated at the front of the first balcony. To those who saw her there, she might have seemed like a glamorous figurehead, a former singing star serenely overseeing the performances. Her life as impresario, however, was anything but serene: Sills had discovered that the role of general director required even more concentration and dedication than the role of prima donna.

When she was not watching performances from her regular seat, Sills was backstage, conferring with the stage crew and bolstering the morale of the singers, or in her office, catching up on paperwork while listening to the opera on her private backstage monitor. Her schedule for a typical day—February 18, 1988, for example— illustrates the diversity of her duties as general director.

On that Thursday morning, she arrived at her office at 7:55. The opera season was almost six months off, but the company's annual season of musicals was scheduled to begin the following week. The dress rehearsal for *The Music Man* would take place that evening. Seated at her desk, Sills read her mail and signed the letters she had dictated the previous day. At 8:45 A.M., she placed a telephone call to Vienna, Austria. Speaking in German, she spent the next half hour making production arrangements for two operas by Austrian composer Alexander von Zemlinsky (1872–1942), which she hoped City Opera could present during the 1990 season. Already tucked into her briefcase were the operas' scores; at the end of the day, she would study them at home so she could decide how to cast them when the time came.

At 9:15 A.M., Sills gave an interview to a reporter from *Musical America* magazine; the subject was the young American composer Jay Reise, whose first opera was scheduled to premiere at City Opera in September 1988. At 10:30, she joined her administrative assistant to discuss fees for 32 singers she hoped to sign up. An hour later, she met with an orchestra representative to negotiate the musicians' rotation system during the musical-comedy season. At 1:00 P.M., she lunched with members of a foundation that wanted to establish a scholarship fund for young American conductors at City Opera.

After lunch, Sills joined the costume designer responsible for *The Ballad of Baby Doe*, which was scheduled for fall production. At 4:30, she discussed fu-

Just after Sills got City Opera back on its feet, a fire destroyed the company's warehouse in Passaic, New Jersey. Thousands of expensive costumes and props were lost.

ture roles with one of the company's baritones. Next, she returned the telephone messages that had accumulated during the day. At 5:45, Muffy Greenough, who had become a graphic artist, arrived with her father to accompany Sills to a cocktail party for an author friend. Following a hasty dinner at a Greenwich Village restaurant, Sills and her daughter returned to the theater for the *Music Man* dress rehearsal. After its conclusion at 11:00 P.M., Sills talked to cast members and the production staff, then headed home. There she studied the Zemlinsky opera scores before catching a few hours of sleep. The following morning, she was back at her City Opera desk by 7:45.

"My social life is a wreck; there isn't any," Sills told an interviewer in early 1988. "When I was a singer, I was always on display, careful about my clothes and hair. Now there's no time to shop, to have my hair done. I gain weight, I lose it. I just don't have the time any more to worry about what I look like. That discipline is gone. My rest is gone. I'm now on four or five hours' sleep. I sleep with a pad and a pen that lights up on the bedside table, and in the middle of the night, when something just dawns on me, I start scribbling on the pad. Sometimes the next morning, I can't even read it!"

Nonetheless, Sills loved her work. She had been delighted when Angel Records remastered and released many of her early recordings in 1985, but she refused to dwell on the past. "Once something is done, it's time to turn the page and move on to something else," she told an interviewer. "Do I want to hear more praise for my singing? No, I did that already." Then, referring to critics who thought her voice thin, even shrill during the last years of her singing career, she asked, "Do I want to hear my singing picked on?" Answering her own question, she said, laughing, "No, I did that already, too!"

Sills's frequent use of the phrase "I did that already" refers to a ring that her husband once gave her. "When Peter gave me a ring inscribed I DID

THAT ALREADY, he was reminding me that just because I had a success at one opera house, I didn't have to repeat it at another. I didn't have to do anything I didn't want to do," Sills recalled in her autobiography.

By the time she reached her late fifties, Sills was weary of the strain of being general director of City Opera. She had hinted at her future, and at the continual pull between her career and her home life, when she wrote *Beverly* in 1987: "I don't know how many more years I'll stay in my job. I think our next general director should be someone who can make at least a 10- or 15-year commitment to City Opera. My idea of the perfect general manager is an unmarried 45-year-old orphan. One of these days, I'd like to spend a little time with my husband. I'm a very liberated woman and I think I'm good at my job, but I'm slowly coming to the realization that I won't have to fuss and worry when it's time for me to vacate that basement office for good. I knew when to stop singing. I think I'll be just as smart when I retire from my job as general director."

On May 11, 1988, the *New York Times* ran a front-page picture of Sills: The former prima donna, reported the newspaper, had announced that she would retire in early 1989. She would remain with City Opera, however, as president of the board of directors. "I would never abandon this company," she told repoters. "It's been my passion all my adult life."

Sills's final show at City Opera, *The Pajama Game*, was greeted with criti-

A beaming Sills stands amid a sea of balloons at her farewell gala at City Opera. "It's impossible," said one admirer, "to be around her and not smile."

cal cheers in February 1989. A revival of a 1954 Broadway hit, the musical was praised for its "lighthearted" approach, for the "power and charm" of its singers, for its conductor's "driving performance," and for the "brilliance" of its sets and costumes. "For *The Pajama Game*, her last production before she retires next week," said the *New York Times* review, "Miss Sills has pulled out all the stops."

Sills's retirement unleashed an outpouring of tributes. Typical were remarks made by television newsman Mike Wallace: "By the sheer power of her down-to-earth personality she has made her art form accessible to many people who otherwise might never have gone near an opera house," he said. "Her spirit is so sunny that it's impossible to be around her and not smile. And although she may be leaving the opera behind, I have a hunch we'll be hearing a good deal more from, and about, Beverly Sills, as the years go on."

Sills assumed her new position as president of the City Opera board of directors in March 1989. Although she was relieved to be rid of the stress of running City Opera, she was glad to be still involved in the future of her beloved company. As for her other careers, "I did that already."

FURTHER READING

Erikson, Helen. *Young Person's Guide to the Opera.* Englewood Cliffs, NJ: Silver Burdett, 1980.

Ewen, David. *The New Encyclopedia of the Opera.* New York: Hill & Wang, 1971.

Jefferson, Alan. *The Glory of Opera.* New York: Putnam, 1976.

Kupferberg, Herbert. *Opera.* New York: Newsweek Books, 1975.

Osborne, Charles. *How to Enjoy Opera.* Ed. Melvyn Bragg. Salem, NH: Merrimac Publishers Circle, 1984.

Paolucci, Bridget. "Remembrance of Recordings Past with Beverly Sills." *Ovation*, April 1985, 14–18.

Robinson, Francis. *Celebration.* New York: Doubleday, 1979.

Saal, Hubert. "The True Story of Beverly Sills." *New York Times Magazine*, 17 September 1967.

Sargeant, Winthrop. "Superstar." *New Yorker*, 6 March 1971, 49–64.

Sills, Beverly and Lawrence Linderman. *Beverly: An Autobiography.* New York: Bantam Books, 1988.

Sills, Beverly. *Bubbles.* New York: Simon & Schuster, 1976.

The Simon & Schuster Book of the Opera. New York: Simon & Schuster, 1977.

Sokol, Martin L. *The New York City Opera.* New York: Macmillan, 1981.

SELECTED DISCOGRAPHY

Donizetti, Gaetano. *Lucia di Lammermoor, The Three Queens.* Angel Records.

Handel, George Frideric. *Giulio Cesare.* EMI Records.

Massenet, Jules. *Manon.* Angel Records.

Moore, Douglas. *The Ballad of Baby Doe.* Deutsche Grammophon.

Verdi, Giuseppe. *La Traviata.* Angel Records.

CHRONOLOGY

May 26, 1929	Born Belle Miriam Silverman in Brooklyn, New York
1933	Appears on "Rainbow House," a New York City radio show
1936	Changes name to Beverly Sills; becomes a regular on nationwide radio show, "Major Bowes' Capitol Family"; begins voice lessons with Estelle Liebling
1944	Tours with Gilbert and Sullivan repertory company
1951	Tours with the Wagner Opera Company
1955	Makes New York City Opera debut in Strauss's *Die Fledermaus*
1956	Marries Peter Greenough; moves to Cleveland, Ohio
1958	Appears in New York City premiere of Moore's *The Ballad of Baby Doe*
1959	Gives birth to daughter, Meredith, known as Muffy
1960	With husband and daughter, moves to Milton, Massachusetts
1961	Gives birth to son, Peter, Jr., known as Bucky
1967	Plays Cleopatra in the New York City Opera production of Handel's *Julius Caesar*
1968	Sings title role in Massenet's *Manon*
1969	Appears in Rossini's *The Siege of Corinth* at La Scala opera house in Milan, Italy; moves with her family to New York City
1970	Portrays Queen Elizabeth I in Donizetti's *Roberto Devereux*; debuts at London's Covent Garden
1971	Performs at the White House at invitation of President Nixon
1974	Undergoes successful cancer surgery
1975	Makes Metropolitan Opera debut in *The Siege of Corinth*
1979	Becomes general director of New York City Opera; makes last performance as prima donna at City Opera
1980	Receives Medal of Freedom from President Carter; performs in farewell gala at City Opera
1985	Sills's recordings are reissued by Angel Records; warehouse fire destroys costumes for New York City Opera
1988	Sills announces retirement as City Opera's general director
1989	Becomes president of the board at City Opera

INDEX

PICTURE CREDITS

Bridget Paolucci is a writer, lecturer, and broadcaster specializing in opera. Her articles have appeared in *Opera News, Musical America,* and *Ovation* magazines, and her music commentary is carried by National Public Radio and the Australian Broadcasting Corporation. Paolucci lectures extensively for the Metropolitan Opera Guild and the New York City Opera Guild. The recipient of a Fulbright grant, she has served as a judge for the Metropolitan Opera Regional Auditions for the past 11 years.

❖   ❖   ❖

Matina S. Horner is president of Radcliffe College and associate professor of psychology and social relations at Harvard University. She is best known for her studies of women's motivation, achievement, and personality development. Dr. Horner serves on several national boards and advisory councils, including those of the National Science Foundation, Time Inc., and the Women's Research and Education Institute. She earned her B.A. from Bryn Mawr College and Ph.D. from the University of Michigan, and holds honorary degrees from many colleges and universities, including Mount Holyoke, Smith, Tufts, and the University of Pennsylvania.